INK

THE INVISIBLE
IES

TEACHING FOR MOTIVATION

SUPER-CHARGED LEARNING THROUGH THE 'INVISIBLE CURRICULUM'

ANDREW HAMMOND

First Published 2016

by John Catt Educational Ltd,
12 Deben Mill Business Centre,
Old Maltings Approach,
Melton, Woodbridge IP12 1BL

Tel: +44 (0) 1394 389850
Fax: +44 (0) 1394 386893
Email: enquiries@johncatt.com
Website: www.johncatt.com

ISBN: 978 1 909717 367

Set and designed by Theoria Design.

Contents

Foreword
by Guy Holloway

This is not a book for those who think in terms of delivering a 'good' or 'outstanding' lesson. It is a clarion call to look far beyond such labels, and indeed to ponder our first responsibilities when developing young minds. This book is a reminder that teaching is a noble profession, and that all great teachers leave a legacy in the hearts and minds of their pupils.

Great teachers have pupils hanging on every word. Their pupils go home and look forward to doing their homework assignment for such teachers. And this is because, through a combination of eye contact, a smile, and ultimately belief in a child, great teachers motivate children to discover their passions and inspire them to become the person that they can be.

The words of the nineteenth-century American writer Henry David Thoreau can be seen as a kind of gauntlet to the teaching profession, 'Most men lead lives of quiet desperation and go the grave with the song still in them.' If true, the tragedy starts at school where systems can, and sometimes do, grind down the effervescent spirit of the child.

Great teachers nurture the heart, instil self-confidence and change the course of a child's life. This book identifies that process and it is as profound and revealing as it is straightforward.

Guy Holloway
Headmaster, Hampton Court House
@GuyHolloway_HCH

1 We don't like to talk about it

Here is a strange story that will stretch the bounds of belief for even the most imaginative reader. But, apparently, it really happened.

Fourteen billion years ago, all the energy that has ever existed and is ever likely to exist in the universe was created inside a bubble smaller than a pinhead. The rapid inflation that happened next, known affectionately and somewhat misleadingly as the 'big bang', saw this little bubble grow from the size of a single atom to the size of a galaxy in a fraction of a second. And it kept expanding. It's still growing today, so I'm told; we're all sailing further away from our neighbours towards... somewhere else, pushing back the black and turning nothingness into somethingness as we go. Before the little pinhead there was nothing and then suddenly there was something. Everything in fact. Matter and energy were with us from that point on. All the energy that has ever existed and will ever exist was created then.

A story that belongs in a kid's sci-fi book, don't you think? But it's a tale that has been passed down by generations of experts and we believe them – of course we do, they're called *scientists*. If a scientist tells you something, you tend to believe it, don't you?

But we don't generally believe in ghosts and we don't believe in spirits and we don't believe in magic. Many of us don't believe in telepathy, nor fortune-telling nor mediums who can contact your late uncle. But we do believe in other things that seem just as incredulous. My mobile phone can bounce a message to me from a friend on the other side of the world, via a satellite in space, in seconds, and we believe it has to do with quantum physics, though few of us will ever see an atom for ourselves. But we believe and trust in the technology – in fact we depend on it. Many of us live our lives around it. Our belief is unshakeable. Yes, of course this text came to us via quantum technology, didn't you know that? I mean, everyone knows *that*. Technological advances that should utterly baffle us are accepted without a second glance.

But stand up in a room full of delegates and start talking about a different invisible force, called 'motivation', and you'll soon encounter some sceptical, even cynical looks. You'll see colour drain from faces, phones coming out of pockets and excuses coming thick and fast for why they really need to be somewhere else. That's if they are present in the first place. If you're competing with a seminar next door on data analysis or preparing for inspection, you'll be lucky to get anyone at all. Getting busy people to believe that motivation matters and is worth discussing can be difficult.

I recently delivered an in-school CPD training day on the subject of motivation in teaching and learning. The night before the event I was emailed by the headteacher. Just a quick note to say how much he was looking forward to my visit and how he hoped my drive up to the school was trouble-free. A charming little missive, I thought, very thoughtful. And then I scrolled down the email to discover the real reason for his message: a large photograph of Mr Motivator, the pink-leotarded gym instructor of *GMTV* fame in the 1980s.

Of course.

I resisted the temptation to turn up in tracksuit and head band, with a large CD player in my hand blurting out Tina Turner's 'Simply the Best'.

Half an hour into my preliminary discussion with the headteacher, in which I was striving to shed light on what did and did not motivate him deep down, his eyes glazed over. I said, "Are you OK?"

He said, "Yes, I'm sorry, I was just racking my brains trying to think who you remind me of. Who was that fellow with the multi-coloured jumpers? You know, used to read people's stars on the telly. What was his name?"

I informed him, somewhat incredulous.

"That's the fellow. Consulting your star charts, aren't you? About to tell me my moon's in Venus, eh?"

"Hmm."

"No?"

"Not exactly," I said.

Facing playful cynicism when broaching the subject of motivation with busy headteachers is not uncommon. I have recently taken on another headship for myself in a school that, according to the good people at Ofsted, requires significant and rapid improvement. So I recognise how the visible stuff can dominate our thoughts, with the imminent prospect of visiting inspectors crunching and munching on your data. Motivation can so easily be confined to the drawer like some junior magic set after Christmas. It's invisible, it's the dark arts and there just aren't enough hours in the day to start delving into people's psyche in search of their mojo when you have to get the reading, writing and maths attainment up. I pay my staff to do a job and they should get on with it. The children all know they have work to do and they should get on with it too. Life would be so much easier if everyone just got on with what they are supposed to do, and stopped checking their equilibrium every five minutes to assess how their current role meets their motivational needs.

And then some bright spark comes along and starts saying that motivation lies at the heart of everything and how none of us are robots and we all have feelings and thoughts, you know.

This entire series is dedicated to the *invisible curriculum* – the skills, traits and attributes we acquire that enable us to become an active and fulfilled member of planet Earth, amongst the families, friends and colleagues with whom we share it. I call these skills, traits and attributes our 'invisible ink'. A school needs these qualities flowing through its corridors like a pen needs ink.

And so, to anyone interested only in visible results, like all titles in this series, *Teaching for Motivation* may be a source of irritation, or a bountiful source of fuel to feed the flames of cynicism and scepticism. Just get on with it – if you want visible results, focus on the visible signs of progress, that usually come in percentages.

But may I make a respectful plea, even to the most hardened cynic, bruised and battle-scarred like me by the challenges of school leadership, to bear with me for just a little while longer? If after reading this book you still feel that motivation should remain in the drawer marked rainy day playtimes, then fair enough. I'll go out and buy a multi-coloured jumper with a knitted sundial on it.

Motivation is not a luxury, nor a whimsical self-indulgence. It's bigger and better than that. It will tip the balance between a good school and an outstanding one. More than that, motivation may be the single most important factor in determining the success of your school. It is the greatest weapon in the war against apathy and defeatism. And as any school leader knows, these can be as corrosive to a staff room as rust to an old car. In the school in which I now find myself, it is self-motivation that will expedite the progress that we know we must make. And it is demotivation that will make the challenge unassailable.

If searching for motivation is, for you, tantamount to consulting your stars then so be it. We are all made of stardust anyway.

But one thing is certain. A self-motivated teacher can light up a class, instil a 'can-do' attitude in everyone and make learning a joy. A self-motivated student will always achieve their potential, but a student who only works and learns because they are told to do so will have a much, much steeper hill to climb when adulthood finally comes. What will drive them to get out of bed and into work in the future? Their salary alone? What an empty life that will be. Without addressing what does and doesn't motivate them deep down, how will they ever know which job to strive for in the first place?

Humans are different to programmed robots on a technical assembly line precisely because we require self-motivation to work at full capacity and to achieve our potential. We can't divorce 'doing' from 'feeling'; every action comes with a feeling too and we'd like it to be a positive one, if possible. It is rare to be able to work at your absolute, full capacity simply because you're paid to, or told to, whether you're an adult or a child.

As leaders, we can incentivise our staff to work harder by dangling the usual carrots – a salary increase, more planning and preparation time, greater roles and responsibilities for their CV, fewer playground duties, more badges to wear. These things may work on some, for some of the time, but the greatest productivity and the highest level of practice, care and attention are seen in the most self-motivated colleagues. And the same is true of children.

It is a truth which cannot be ignored that what seems invisible at first may have the greatest influence on the visible signs of what we term 'achievement' in a school, whether that be end of Key Stage results, sporting caps, or musical performances. The energy and productivity that comes from the self-motivated person surpasses that seen in the coerced or extrinsically motivated, surely. And when a team is motivated, there is no limit to what their combined synergy can accomplish. Provided they have *something to believe in* (I will return to this key element again).

So is it possible to make someone self-motivated? It seems a contradiction, doesn't it? You *will* be motivated to finish this piece of work, or mark those books or perform in this production with a smile on your face. Won't you!?

What you can do, and what this book will guide you towards, is to create the conditions in which a person feels disposed to be intrinsically motivated. And that is possible. But first you need to know what motivates a teacher or a child, because we are not all motivated by the same aspirations or activities. This, surely, is one of the most important tasks for a teacher – to help her students identify what motivates them, deep down. It has taken me many years to realise that achieving what you want is almost always possible; it's *knowing* what you want that's the hard part.

The clue to understanding what you want out of your career lies in identifying what does and does not motivate you inside. A good school presents enough different opportunities within a rich curriculum to enable a child, and his teacher, to discover where their intrinsic motivation lies. They *will* find it, eventually, and this book may assist.

As ever in this series, I am delving into the invisible nature of learning and development, far beyond the naked eye or the assessment radar. No wonder that motivation can be greeted with suspicion at best, derision at worst; *you can't see it*.

But this particular book comes at the invisible curriculum from a different angle; other titles shed light on the invisible skills, attitudes and aptitudes which children pick up along the learning journey, and I call this their 'invisible ink'. Whilst learning from the visible curriculum – the knowledge, skills and concepts laid down in a school syllabus – children also learn how to learn, how to think, how to create, how to collaborate, and so on. But this particular book concentrates not on what they gain out of the process of schooling, but what they *invest in it*. Get the motivation right and you'll enable them to gain the most benefit from everything else. Put the children in a motivated predisposition to learn and they will learn a great deal. Perhaps it should have come first in the series, for motivation of the kind that is homegrown, deep inside the gut, will be the driving force for deep and meaningful learning. It harnesses our energy, gets the invisible ink flowing.

And just as importantly, we need to create coping strategies for areas that are positively demotivating for students and teachers – because we can't all busy ourselves only with the things that we find motivating. But what is fascinating to watch, in children and teachers alike, is how engagement in highly motivating activities has a positive impact on all aspects of learning. We know this to be true. A child who derives deep satisfaction and high levels of energy from working in 'their element' will bring self-confidence and a positive attitude to other aspects of their daily work too.

In search of motivation...

It has become something of a western obsession, perhaps, to rationalise everything, to try to reason it out using deductive logic in our heads. Much of our curriculum, after all, is devoted to developing children's powers of reason and deduction. What does *this* mean? How can we understand *that*? How can this be explained, rationally? How can we conceptualise this and so understand it more deeply? We spend so much time living in our heads, and using our bodies as receptacles for getting our brains from one lesson to the next, it is a wonder any of us can get out of a chair by the time we graduate.

But self-motivation lies in the gut. It is impervious to the usual logical reasoning and analysing that happens so much of the time in school. It's a gut reaction. The energy that emanates from the self-motivated person comes not from the head; it is the 'fire in the belly'.

Think of a time when you felt such a fire in your belly, either when you were at school as a student yourself, or in your adult life – that moment when you felt so absorbed in something, so engaged, so committed to what you were doing. The fashionable term 'in flow-state' is often used these days to describe the act of being so absorbed in something that you lose a sense of time and place, and a creative drive takes hold. In book two, *Teaching for Creativity*, I called this 'creactivity'. But it needn't be creative at all; it might be when you are cycling or swimming or nursing an animal, tending a garden or just doing a Sudoku. These are often the moments that find us in 'our element'.

At these times it is our *motivation* that drives us on. It is the glue that binds us to the project and enables us to see it through. Perhaps filing it in the same drawer as the junior magic set was apt – it is indeed a form of magical stardust which, when sprinkled onto our efforts, can improve them immeasurably.

But it's invisible and it relies on having something to believe in.

This book will help you to do a number of things:

1. Identify what does and does not motivate your staff and pupils;

2. Understand the importance of having a vision – something for your staff to believe in;

3. Create a climate in which their self-motivation can flourish;

4. Improve communication so that you are communicating with colleagues and pupils in the language of their motivations;

5. Reduce apathy and improve attendance and engagement in school life; and

6. Monitor and track the self-motivation of everyone in the school community.

The pre-ordaining 'big bang' theory aside, there do seem to be times in our lives when we have more energy or less energy. You can see it in the children too. There are times when they want to work so hard their tongues dribble and they look fit to burst. I call it the 'veins factor' – when a child tells you so excitedly what he's doing that you can see the veins stand out in his neck.

Don't you just love those high-octane moments of engagement – when you set a child a challenge, pass him a baton so appealing that he runs with it like an Olympic sprinter? It seems like they have gained new energy from somewhere and it's a pleasure to see. It may have been a piece of work, an independent project perhaps, or something artistic, musical or sporting. It may have been a public presentation that set his energy flowing, the chance to speak in assembly, or maybe an audition for a leading role in a school play. Who knows what gets these kids' energy flowing? But when these moments come, they are not only felt and experienced in the head; they are felt in the gut. Though the effects of high motivation can be seen in our eyes, the source of it lies in our bellies.

Adult staff are no different, I find, although they make take a little longer to believe in visions.

And that's just the point of this book. It may be invisible – as all the important things in school are; like character, creativity or curiosity, those qualities that make up children's 'invisible ink' – but motivation is the very best fuel to produce some turbo-charged learning in the classroom. I hope this book will help you to achieve this. It may even help you find your own motivation too, if you haven't already done so. The fact that you have voluntarily purchased this book may give you an indication of where your motivation lies, unless you were coerced into reading it by a line-manager who values your motivation, in which case, you are in safe hands.

2 Perspectives: teaching for motivation

Measure for measure

We see an odd dichotomy in schools. There is always the need to make and show *progress* – this is the *raison d'être* for any school, especially if you have an inspection looming. Demonstrating that the children are making progress is vitally important in order for a school to prove it is not failing, or coasting. Showing progress means measuring progress, and here's the conundrum: for children to make real progress they need to be motivated and they need to have a fully motivated teacher. But the task of showing progress – through tracking and recording and reporting data – is in itself demotivating for many teachers, though perhaps not all. And the task of sitting tests in order to demonstrate progress is demotivating for most children too. So the very system we have made to show progress may be affecting the quality of that progress itself – because it demotivates many of the teachers and pupils involved in it. How ironic, though not altogether surprising, it is that if you want teachers to inspire and motivate their pupils to make progress, don't ask them to spend all their time tracking and recording and reporting on that progress. In the end, it will lead to a downward trend.

I am facing such a dilemma right now in the school which I have recently taken on. Do I push and push at the data, making sure everyone knows how low it is in certain subjects and year groups, and how it needs to improve, or do I focus more on the drivers that will motivate staff and pupils to improve, which are unlikely to be tasks like measuring data? Should I lead with a data headline and scare everyone into improving? Or should I lead with a different title and hope there is a knock-on effect on the data? It has been suggested to me that one way to make rapid progress is to place Venn diagrams and charts and tables all over the walls of the staff room. This will keep people's minds focused. It may do that, but I'm not sure what it will do for their motivation.

I am certain that a highly motivated and collegiate staff will move the school and the children on towards better progress. But each time I mention the data and the need to show progress, I detect a discernible lowering of shoulders and chins in the common room. We need to be braver than that.

It's back to the embarrassingly obvious cliché once again, involving a pig and a set of scales. Neither the pig nor the farmer are motivated by a weighing session. And what's the point in weighing a pig if you haven't fed it properly?

I wonder how much of our time in schools is spent discussing how we monitor and track learning compared with how much time we spend discussing the learning itself. How much time is spent discussing the pig-weighing equipment? In this 'world without levels' that we are now entering (which is no more than a 'world without numbers' as far as I can see – levels are just expressed in words now) we find ourselves spending hours and hours after school discussing how and when we are going to show progress now that everything has changed. In fact, we spend as much time discussing how we are going to show progress as we spend planning for the kind of inspirational teaching that will see the children making progress in the first place.

None of this is particularly motivating, I find, at least not to me.

But as with so many aspects of education, it is not *either/or*, it is *and*, or it will be once we all sort out how we're going to do it. It is not a question of *either* talking about data *or* talking about quality-first teaching practices, it is *both*. Once we have our new systems for tracking progress in place, and the new nomenclature for attainment is embedded properly across the school (which are simply levels by a different name, as far as I'm concerned) then we will be able to focus too on inspirational, motivational teaching. And I will be able to allow my staff more time to do the things that motivate them again, which for many (though not for all) does not involve number crunching, RAG rating, or ascertaining the subtle shades of difference between one level descriptor and the next (except they are not called levels, they are steps or mileposts or stages, nowadays); rather it is filling children with self-belief, a growth mindset and the motivation to improve.

School: a motivating environment?

In order to encourage that all-important progress, we may often promise rewards in school. And some children work very well for the promise of stars, house points or merits; we can even dangle the prospect of a headteacher's certificate for good work or a mention in the school newsletter. But this will only work for the child who is motivated by such acclaim, and many children simply aren't. Some may find such public recognition positively demotivating. Others may realise that a slip of blue or green paper with 'house point' written across it, after all, is just a slip of paper with words on it. It has little currency in their 'real' lives. If you are a child motivated by being part of a winning team, then it can help, but even then a single house point for good work is hardly going to win the cup for the entire house.

Years of teaching have taught me that the child who is motivated by prizes and cups and recognition is ideally suited to formal education. It was designed for them. But I have also learned that only a small number of children actually are. So what of the others? What motivates them? Why do some children beam at the prospect of a smiley face or an A grade or a round of applause in assembly, while others simply shrug their shoulders and eye you suspiciously if you dare to praise them in public?

In previous titles in this series I have suggested that the current education system is predicated on the following historical assumptions about the purpose of schooling:

1. The most effective way to bring about success for a society and its economy is to develop the *intelligence* of its younger generation.

2. The most accurate measure of intelligence, and therefore a predictor of future success, both for the individual and for the economy, is *academic qualification*.

3. The best way to incentivise students to study for academic qualifications is through a system of external *rewards and sanctions*, and the best way to chart their progress is by *examination*.

From a motivation perspective, the unintended consequence of these assumptions is that we also assume that all children are motivated by the rewards on offer in the classroom. These rewards usually, though not always, consist of recognising good work with the aforementioned stars, merits, and so on. Every school I've ever worked in, or visited as an educational consultant, has a formal system for this, either wrapped up in a Marking & Feedback Policy, a Behaviour Policy or a Rewards & Sanctions Policy, or enshrined in the Code of Conduct that is adhered to across the school. Achieve well in class and you'll get noticed; being noticed for high attainment is a good thing; praise from the teacher is a good thing; recognition from the headteacher for extraordinary achievement is a brilliant thing too. This is what children are conditioned into believing.

There are children for whom this is enough. They will work their socks off to be top of the class, or to feature in the honours list or have their work displayed on the excellence board in the school's reception or the headteacher's office. If only all children were motivated in this way. But even if they were, this is a dubious precedent to set for adult life and all its challenges. In many jobs there is no notion of 'top of the class'. And how will they work as part of a team if they spent their schooling striving to be top of the class?

Are we at risk of conditioning the children into believing there will always be a prize if you do well? Does being a good husband earn you a prize? Will there be a certificate in my letter box one day, saying 'this is to certify that Andrew Hammond has been a good husband'? I doubt it very much. How does an A star in history make you a better mother? Does an E in geography disqualify you from being a good uncle? Will showing care and consideration to a friend in need earn you a certificate? Is that why you do it?

As an employee, will doing a good job always earn you a mention in the company's newsletter? Of course not, though it may earn you the adult equivalent of house points – money. In some ways, house points are handed out in schools like pocket money, and to some children they are worth as much. But the currency plummets for the child who isn't interested in the slip of blue, red, yellow or green paper handed to him that will ultimately lead to his house winning the bit of silverware for the term. So what? What's really in it for him? And what if a piece of work he is particularly proud of slips through the net and is not recognised by that magical bit of paper or a badge, or a star on a board, or being moved from the rain cloud to the sunshine on the wall display behind him?

I have met many adults who are motivated by earning big bucks in their workplace and this works very well for them. Needless to say, as an educationalist, I have never possessed such a motivator. That doesn't make me a better person or a worse person. I feel no piety or smugness because I'm driven by different motivators in my working life, rather than earning more money. I am just different, and consequently poorer, at least financially speaking. But I cannot complain about that. I wasn't going for the dollars, I was striving for something else. In my case, I am motivated by making a difference, learning new knowledge and passing it on to others. This is precisely why I teach and write books. I am where I need to be, though not without considerable soul searching, questioning and the endless self-doubt that consumes many people like me – and I think some of this struggle has been due to the conditioning I endured as a pupil, which said we should all be amassing house points like money.

At school I wasn't driven by the prospect of gaining more house points than anyone else, or by having the most expensive cricket bat or shoes or pencil case. But some of my friends were. I didn't feel inferior to them, and neither did I think they were inferior to me. Where some were thrilled if their story writing earned them a star in class, I was thrilled if my story writing satisfied me – if it turned out the way I'd envisioned it. I didn't care if it earned me a star or a house point or a pat on the head; I did it to satisfy me. And consequently my bedroom was littered with screwed up bits of unfinished stories and poems which dissatisfied me, whether they were held to be 'good' or not. Mine was a more frustrating existence, and it still is.

This is why I believe that the current system of education, predicated on those historical assumptions and the sanctions and rewards that follow, lends itself very well to the child who is motivated by rewards, and the rare child who, sadly, is motivated only by avoiding punishment. Extrinsic prizes and punishments do little for intrinsic motivation, by definition. Such methods of incentivising children to work hard may alter the reason why they do it in the first place, thus affecting their motivation. As Alfie Kohn (1999) says in his superb book, *Punished by Rewards*:

> Rewards are often successful at increasing the probability that we will do something. At the same time, though, they also change the way we do it. They offer one particular reason

for doing it, sometimes displacing other possible motivations.
And they change the attitude we take towards the activity. In
each case, by any reasonable measure, the change is for the
worse. (Kohn, 1999: 35)

Kohn hits the nail on the head; and I have often made a similar point in
the context of creativity in particular – that children will create, create,
create when they have something they desperately want to express. They
will be less prolific, ultimately, if they are creating only because they've been
told to do so in an art lesson or a story-writing class. But appeal to their
imagination and they will be self-motivated to create, because now they
have something they must express. The same is true of learning – appeal to
the children's *curiosity* and they will learn more effectively and prolifically
than through rewards and sanctions only. The reward lies in satisfying their
burning curiosity – the natural fuel that drives all learning on and reels in
the attention of the children. Rewards and sanctions cannot compete when
the child *wants* to learn in order to satisfy their curiosity. The key is to reveal
the learning objectives in such a way that appeals to their curiosity in the first
place! Perhaps this is why I so often liken a lesson to a good chapter in a story:
it has an exciting opener, some punchy dialogue, pace, vivid imagery and a
slow revealing of the plot.

But this is all getting dangerously close to the old joke: How many motivational
coaches does it take to change a light bulb? Only one, but the light bulb needs to
want to change.

I know, as a practising teacher and school leader, that you can't sit around waiting
for all children to *want* to learn for themselves. You can't wait for them all to feel
the fire in the belly and if they don't, just tell them, "Never mind, in a minute
we'll go onto something else that will interest you instead." The light bulb may
not want to change sometimes, but you've still got to change it. Children may not
feel motivated to complete a page of maths sums or a reading comprehension or
a painting or a two-mile cross-country run, no matter how much you dress it up
in storytelling language. But they still have to do it.

This leads me to an important pre-condition for teaching for motivation, and it
may seem counter-intuitive. It is as follows, and if all children could grasp it early
on in their educational career, things would be a lot easier for them:

School is about hard work. Get used to it.

It is a bitter pill to swallow, perhaps, and it isn't remotely motivational, but it is a truth worth emphasising, regardless of what truly motivates a child, or teacher for that matter. Once we can accept this truth, then, and only then, can we open Pandora's box and start delving around for what does or does not motivate a child deep down. Whatever we find, whether it is painting or playing or writing or dancing or making new friends, it will never be the only activity that child will do in school. So the overarching maxim must always be that school is a place in which you must work hard and try your best, whatever the subject or discipline. Like dishes on a sushi conveyor belt, your favourite will come around, you will engage with something that fills your belly with fire once in a while. But you must be hungry for it when it comes, you must already be working hard, this is the key point. You can't have a piecemeal school experience, only dipping into the things that intrigue you and saying 'pass' to the others.

I assume that the rewards and sanctions in place in a school are designed to achieve just that, and every school needs them. But central to this book is the idea that although children find some subjects or activities more motivating than others, there are ways in which we can teach them, ways in which we can create a climate for the children, across the curriculum, that will appeal to their intrinsic motivators no matter what the subject. They won't have to endure a diet of demotivating activity four-and-a-half days a week just for the motivating experiences available to them on one afternoon. If we can identify their intrinsic motivators accurately, we can meet their needs at all times through:

● the way we demonstrate motivational behaviour to them

● the language we use when talking to them

● the learning groups and pairings we put them in

● the enticing challenges we set them and the choices we give them

● the way we observe and report on their motivational behaviour

These strategies are not subject-specific. They are generic, cross-curricular approaches. They cater for all sorts of motivational types. They are the learning conditions which I refer to throughout this series and they will be as useful to us in this book as they were in previous titles, precisely because they address the invisible curriculum, where motivation lies, along with character, creativity and so on.

You can't teach someone else to be motivated, but you can create the conditions in which they feel disposed to be motivated. And you can try to learn more about what motivates them particularly.

And the fun part is, they may not yet know what motivates themselves, and neither may their parents. 'What motivates you?' is not a question often asked in school, except in anger or frustration at a non-compliant child who seems reticent most of the time and refuses to work or get to school in the first place. But it is a question which is fundamental to getting the most out of all children, and their teachers, enabling them to find their true potential. Until you ask the question, you will be getting just a fraction of the real child, and it won't be their best.

So how do you ask it? And what kind of answer will you get?

Identifying intrinsic motivators

Long before he stood shoulder-to-shoulder with his father, my eldest son asked me the following question:

"What will I be when I'm older, Dad?"

After careful thought – because I know how a parent's influence can serve as a self-fulfilling prophecy sometimes – I decided to dodge the ball and said,

"Happy, son. You'll be happy when you're older."

This was probably even worse than saying a vet or an actor or a train driver, because to set my children on a quest for happiness is a daft task, but there we are. Happiness comes when you don't go looking for it, I find.

"How will I know when I'm happy?" he said. A brilliant question.

I said, "What makes you happy now?"

He said, "Chocolate."

"Anything else?"

"X Box."

"Hmm… anything else?"

He said, "Adventures and things."

"OK," I said, "Now that sounds interesting. So you like adventures? And isn't school an adventure?"

"No."

"But you learn new things there every day, and that's a kind of adventure, isn't it?"

"No."

"No?"

"No, Dad. It's boring."

"OK. Well when you're older you'll be doing something that you don't find boring, I'm sure."

"How will I know what that is?"

"It will be something that motivates you," I said.

"What will that be?"

"Well, what motivates you in school now?" I asked.

"Dunno. Never really thought about it."

"Hasn't anyone asked you?"

"Nope."

And I don't suppose they have. The system isn't really set up to ask that question. Even when it comes to careers advice, I wonder if we focus too much on the skills and attributes we show in school – the grades especially – and then source some career options that neatly fit with them. The skills and attributes my children demonstrate may well suggest certain careers, but this is only half the story. What will bring lasting success and fulfilment will not be their skills, not even their character; it will be through knowing what motivates them and doing that.

It is logical to suggest that to be a vet you need good sciences; to be a lawyer you need good literacy and perhaps a knowledge and appreciation of Latin; or for an accountant you need good maths. These are gross over-simplifications and somewhat stereotypical too! Of course, you need other attributes too and, most of all, you need the motivation to do this kind of work in the first place. If you have the intrinsic motivation, the fire in the belly, you can do pretty much anything, because you will be determined to get the grades, hone the skills and, crucially, get out of bed each morning to get to work. You have the *vision*.

The most numerate of accountants or the most literate of lawyers do not get out of bed and off to work because of their skills alone. The thing that drives them to rise from their slumber and earn is their *motivation*. If their intrinsic motivators match the kind of experiences and challenges they are presented with at work then they are in the right job, in their element. If they don't, they may not be, and, like many people, the need to earn money will become conflated with their motivation. Millions of people may well be in the wrong job but they do it because they have a mortgage and some loans and a family and some holidays booked and little or no opportunity to retrain as something else. Perhaps that's what I should have said to my son – "You'll be doing a job which pays the bills, son. Any more questions? Right, finish your tea."

Such a response would have been defeatist and I am not in the habit of demotivating my children, any more than the pupils I teach or the staff I have the privilege of leading. I want them to see possibilities rather than glass ceilings. I want them to strive for what they want – but to do that they need to know what they want in the first place. As I have said earlier, this is the hardest question, but clues to the answer may lie in our intrinsic motivators.

So what motivates you as a person working in education? The possibilities are endless, of course, but browse the following assortment and see if anything takes your fancy. I regularly visit schools to work with staff to find their motivations and these are the drivers which I find most common.

INTRINSIC MOTIVATORS FOR TEACHERS AND SCHOOL LEADERS
Making a difference – having a moral purpose and something to believe in
Knowledge and expertise – learning new knowledge and passing it on to others
Creating new ideas and solving problems
Friendship and camaraderie among colleagues
Job security – a planned and predictable future

Autonomy – having the freedom to make your own decisions and act on them
Recognition and praise – receiving positive feedback and public acclaim
Leading and managing others, delegating and overseeing
Monetary gain – having the latest gadgets and possessions

These are not hierarchical. But it is interesting that I have placed making a difference at the top and earning big bucks at the bottom. Any one of these is of great value to some people and not any one is 'best'. You may be motivated by a number of these things; you may be de-motivated by others. For myself, making a difference and knowledge and expertise are very important to me and they provide a good reason to get out of bed and into work, but as I have said earlier, this does not make me a better person than the colleague who gets out of bed in order to earn money and buy the latest gadget. Being motivated by learning new knowledge does not make me a clever person particularly, it just keeps me motivated. It is a pity that making a difference to others' lives and earning money for yourself do seem to be mutually exclusive aims sometimes. The hard-working nurse, aid worker or carer will not, I suspect, be rushing out to buy the latest Maserati, because society doesn't value these jobs, in monetary terms, as highly as others I could mention. But they do their jobs anyway for the rewards that they bring. People don't often set out on a path to becoming a teacher in order to build their bank account, no matter how relatively secure the education profession may be.

Making friends at work, enjoying camaraderie, is not especially motivating for me. That is not to say I am unfriendly or uncaring – far from it, I hope. I am driven by making a difference to others' lives and by placing the needs of the children at the centre of everything I do, so I don't feel particularly unfriendly. However, I don't go to my workplace for the friendship it offers, I go to work to work. Staff Christmas parties are difficult for me as I don't really know how to make small talk. I am that colleague who, in the midst of the festive spirit, will start talking shop and turn what I regarded hitherto as a frivolous conversation into a meaningful, productive one, albeit one with fewer and fewer people, usually. I don't know how else to behave. I have a few close friends outside school and I enjoy their company enormously. But I understand that other colleagues may go to work partly to see other workmates and enjoy a catch up over coffee break. These are the people who notice when morale is low, and we need them. I am not a curmudgeonly old Scrooge, I just can't think of anything to say at work other than work-related stuff. And some people don't like it when I do that.

A planned and predictable future is not something that motivates me either; in fact I find it demotivating. I have often waited until everything is sorted, everything is cosy and comfortable in my career before then going off in search of a new challenge. This is because creativity and problem-solving are hugely motivating for me; comfort zones are not. While others are change-averse, I am change-friendly to the point of fidgetiness, as anyone who knows me will recognise. I strive for new problems to solve, new challenges, new difficulties to embrace. This does not make me a better person or a worse person. If anything it is a hindrance until a challenge comes along and then I am in my element again. Perhaps this is why I enjoy working in schools so much: you never know what each day will bring. When I reach the stage when things are starting to get comfortable, predictable and easy, that is when the fidgetiness starts again and I want new problems to solve and difficulties to tackle.

Perhaps this is also why, after seventeen years working in independent prep schools, I have recently taken on a headship in a primary academy currently in special measures. I needed a new challenge. As I suspected, the need to show progress and thus pore over data is all-consuming, but it is still about motivation, because schools are about people, essentially. And nowhere will you find a greater need for something to believe in than a school that is judged by Ofsted as 'failing'.

Identifying and reporting on motivation

Do any of these driving forces sound familiar to you? Do you find the discomfort of difficult challenges somewhat addictive, as many teachers and school leaders do? Or do you find constant change and problem-solving impede your teaching and you need a predictable and planned future in order to be at your best? Neither way is better, neither is worse. Perhaps you are most motivated by managing others, delegating tasks and monitoring performance?

The question is, how do you really know?

This is a question that has interested me for many years. How do we really know what we should or shouldn't be doing during our working hours in order for us to feel a proper sense of accomplishment and satisfaction? I have tried to reason this out many times but only recently have realised that motivation lies not in the head but in the gut. I have Mark Turner to thank for this.

I met Mark at an educational conference for school leaders a couple of years ago. I was delivering a seminar on developing creativity across the curriculum; Mark was speaking on the subject of motivation in staff.

He was excellent. Not only was his delivery engaging and motivational, the topic of his talk was intriguing too. He introduced us to a tool for identifying our intrinsic motivators. I resisted the temptation to make an excuse to be elsewhere in order to avoid any sitting on the carpet and searching our souls. No navel-gazing for me. But there was no Tina Turner playing and Mark wasn't wearing a tracksuit and head band, or a multi-coloured jumper, so the signs looked positive.

Mark talked about making communication more effective, improving the efficacy of teams and raising staff morale. These sounded like reasonable aims to have as a school leader and so I turned off my phone, parked my cynicism, and listened in.

Ten years ago Mark's colleague, James Sale, devised something called the Motivational Map™. Inspired by Edgar Schein's *Career Anchors*, Maslow's hierarchy of needs and the personality tool, The Enneagram, Sale's Motivational Map™ works on the premise that we all have the same capacity for motivation – we have the same potential motivators inside us, but we prioritise them differently, depending on our wants and needs and the circumstances in which we find ourselves.

Sale identified nine such motivators, common in us all, but ranked uniquely differently. He put them into three clusters, Growth, Achievement and Relationships:

Group 1: Growth (Self)	
	Searcher: meaning, purpose, benefit
	Spirit: independence, decisions, choices
	Creator: creativity, originality, problem-solving

Group 2: Achievement (Work)	
	Expert: knowledge, training , mastery
	Builder: money, possessions, rewards
	Director: responsibility, influence, control

Group 3: Relationships	
	Star: Recognition, admiration, acclaim
	Friend: Relationships, connection, being valued
	Defender: Security, stability, accuracy

Figure 1: Motivational Map™ by James Sale ©

Now, I'm as sceptical as the next person, as I hope I have made clear already. The moment we start making definitive lists I begin to question whether we can all fit so neatly into them. Few of us like to feel we are a certain 'type' or can be encapsulated by one label or another. And surely aren't we all composite mixes of all of these motivators? It's like saying we are a visual learner rather than a kinesthetic one! Do you remember the fashion for VAK teaching and learning? Surely we are combinations of all types, are we not, though I accept we may have a preferred style. Suggesting to an eight year old that he is a visual learner will mean he is unlikely to try listening ever again. Isn't the same true of these labels too? We are mixtures of them all.

But that's just the point, and the genius of Sale's creation. It is not only your top motivator or your lowest motivator that makes you *you*; it is the unique combination of the ranking of these motivators from 1st to 9th that is intriguing. It is how they are ranked in your profile that gives insight into how and why you act, react and communicate the way you do. And this is ascertained through Sale's Motivational Map™ questionnaire. Sale built an online survey with forty-five questions, underpinned by years of research and some impressive algorithms. The questions seem random at first, especially after too much rationalising. But if our true motivators lie in the gut rather than in the head, then it is better to go with one's gut reaction to such questions and not try to reason them out. One's first response is usually the correct one and will lead to the most honest of reports. We must guard against the usual pondering over whether our first impulse is the 'correct' one; it will be.

As you may have already guessed, I put myself through the process soon after meeting Mark Turner and hearing his motivational speech. When the questionnaire was complete and the Motivational Map™ was presented to me, I was astonished when I saw the most accurate description of me that I had ever seen. Far more accurate than I had hitherto gleaned from school reports or appraisals and such like. My wife read it too and she agreed, it was me alright. It explained a great deal in my career in education to date, which has spanned twenty years, has included several schools, many different roles, over forty books published and over a hundred CPD courses delivered and conference seminars given. My top motivator is Expert and my second highest is Creator: I like learning new knowledge and passing it on, and I like presenting myself with new challenges and new problems to solve. I am happiest when trying to fathom things that are unfamiliar to me. My lowest motivator is Builder, my second lowest is Friend and my third lowest is Defender. It all kind of made sense.

Mark Turner worked with James Sale to adapt the Motivational Maps™, which Sale had been using with adults and organisations with great success, into a student version for application in schools and for parents. The result is an excellent way of providing a 'script' for monitoring and reporting on the children's motivation at school and at home. It helps children to find their element, wherever that may lie.

Needless to say, I soon put my own four children through the process. Again, the results were astonishingly accurate and worth knowing. Both of my boys have Friend as their top motivator. The Motivational Youth Map™ offers advice for how to keep the children motivated. Two such nuggets of advice for Friends, for example, are: always use their name when talking to them, they will feel known and valued by you; and never use sarcasm with them, they will find it very demotivating. This is absolutely true of my boys.

One of my two daughters has Director as her top motivator, and this explains why she is always so thrilled when given the captaincy of a sports team or some responsibility in class such as a group leader role. My other daughter has Creator as her top motivator and this explains why her bedroom, the kitchen, the living room and the dining room are all filled with her paints, her pencils, her works of art, her construction kits and her fashion dolls with their respective mini-wardrobe collections. She is, like her father, at home to chaos and reels against any semblance of order. Provided she is creating, she's happy. Woe betide anyone who tells her to stop playing and clear up.

Why don't my children's teachers know this? Imagine how much more effective communication between them and my children would be if they had this kind of information available? Why don't all teachers know this about their pupils? This would not lead to copious and unwieldy differentiating of every single task provided, or a mixture of teaching styles so complex it would be undeliverable; it simply means that a motivational profile for each child would help their teachers to 'know them better' and that must be a good thing, surely. I have often said in CPD training sessions that 'knowing your pupils like their parents know them' leads to better teaching and learning.

Enhanced teaching and learning

I have shared such personal experiences and details not as a self-indulgence, I hope, but in the expectation that some of the above will ring familiar bells for the reader. You will know colleagues, and pupils, who demonstrate such motivators. You may even recognise yourself in these behaviours and proclivities. Whether you like and trust the Motivational Map is not so important; what matters is that you take time to consider what truly motivates *you*.

Motivation is a curious, capricious and variable thing, like so many of the human traits and attributes that distinguish us from other species, or computers. I have often strived to shed light on that which is invisible but which matters very much in school and beyond. My extensive work in the field of creativity in education has been part of this crusade. I have always been fascinated by how we can accurately show the invisible progress and development which children make beyond their visible grades. Sale and Turner have achieved this: they have provided a script with which school leaders can monitor and report on teachers' teaching performance and with which teachers can monitor and report on their pupils' learning performance. Their Motivational Map™ offers a blueprint for where the energy lies in a teacher and a learner.

I have since become a trained practitioner for the Motivational Maps™ and I now deliver the Maps and CPD training on motivation in schools and other organisations from businesses to charities. Shedding light on what is intrinsically motivating for others, or on what has been causing them irritation and bringing feelings of apathy, has been truly fascinating and I am grateful to Mark for his coaching. (I hope you'll forgive a brief advertisement: www.hammond-consulting.co.uk)

In Figure 2 below, I offer a guide for teachers on how they may find opportunities at work that will boost their motivation, once they know what their lead motivators are, using the Motivational Map™. As many of us know from our work in assessing progress in school, it is not so much the results that matter, it is what you do with them next, and the same is true for motivation: knowing what motivates you is only the beginning, it's the steps that follow that matter if you are to maintain your motivation or, with luck, raise it still further. The following is based on my years in schools, working with colleagues and seeing what does and does not motivate them. James Sale's nomenclature allows me to put a framework around this experience.

Motivator	Description	Opportunities at work
Searcher	· likes to feel what they are doing is important and has value · wants to improve things · likes to see the bigger picture · always interested in pedagogy and the latest practice · can be a little disorganised · dislikes routine, prefers variety · insatiably curious	· curriculum design, assessment coordination, timetabling · writing and reviewing academic policies · school/department development plan · assemblies and talks · guest speakers for enrichment PSHE and spiritual, moral and cultural initiatives
Spirit	· prefers some degree of autonomy to make independent decisions and introduce ideas · a fast thinker, able to see the bigger picture · prefers to work alone · needs positive feedback · can be disorganised so needs deadlines and limits set	· managing a department · teaching in the performing arts · managing own classroom layout and resources · running own clubs and teams · introducing new initiatives for which they can be responsible · running holiday camps and after-school activities
Creator	· highly motivated by new projects, new problems to solve · enjoys creating new things · copes well with change, dislikes routine, can feel bored quickly · high levels of perseverance · needs to feel the 'play buzz' to be engaged and motivated · energetic and hard working	· overseeing displays · staging performances and presentations · whole school events and projects · prospectus and promotional material · creating bespoke teaching and learning resources · exploring ways of integrating technology into learning
Expert	· highly motivated by latest pedagogy and practice · likes the opportunity to share knowledge and expertise · dislikes repetition, prefers to move on to new things quickly · wants to pursue training opportunities · enjoys learning new methods · can appear impatient at times	· overseeing staff CPD · delivering staff INSET · conducting lesson observations · managing school resources · attending CPD courses and disseminating knowledge gained · running parent workshops on supporting their children's learning · learning a new hobby/instrument every school year!

Builder	• motivated by financial incentives and promotions • highly motivated by the latest gadgets, including learning tools and equipment in class • needs to see regular and reliable income coming in • likes to set clear goals can be highly competitive	• pursuing promotions and extra roles and responsibilities • promoting and marketing the school • setting clear goals and challenges • writing career plans and goals • attending CPD courses and teacher events to network and build career profile
Director	• wants to be leading a team or working party • thrives on responsibility and managing others • needs to set goals and devise strategies for achieving them • enjoys upholding school teaching standards wants to be able to show expertise and authority	• managing a department • overseeing a school resource (e.g. library/sports facility) • writing the timetable • chairing committees • carrying out lesson observations • conducting appraisals • training NQTs • staff induction and support
Star	• needs to be recognised for contribution at school • enjoys lead role in projects • thrives on competition and striving to be the best • likes to set themselves goals for what they want to achieve • ambitious and focused	• running assemblies and talks • delivering staff CPD twilights • entering competitions and quizzes • staging whole school events • directing performing arts projects • delivering inspiring lessons • managing sports teams
Friend	• enjoys being a valued member of the team • seeks camaraderie at work • enjoys positive relationships with students • keen to build trust of pupils/parents • needs continuity and proper time to prepare for any change	• staff social committee • school listener • mentor for NQTs • overseeing staff induction • welcoming new pupils • pastoral care • parent/teacher association • teaching social skills and empathy

Defender	• needs to feel well-prepared and organised • prefers routine and can feel unsettled by unplanned change • enjoys working on plans and preparations • requires clear deadlines and timescales • enjoys working with systems	• managing resources and supplies • overseeing budget plans • health and safety officer • risk management officer for trips • pastoral roles and responsibilities • reviewing and editing school policies • embedding technology to improve systems and processes at school, improving efficiency

Figure 2: A guide to finding more motivation at work

I do not believe that an extra management increment on their salary will motivate all teachers; such additional responsibilities carry relatively little pay increases after tax deductions anyway. For the extra work involved, one would rarely take on extra responsibilities in a school for the money alone; there is usually something else that encourages staff to take on more work, and it is often because the nature of the work appeals to their intrinsic motivations.

Every school leader will want their staff to be self-motivated. Knowing what does or does not motivate a teacher will help the headteacher to deploy them in the right roles and in the right key stage. The teacher who is highly motivated by creativity, for example, may readily take on the role of being responsible for public area display boards, without worrying too much if the task brings extra pennies or not; as I have said, the amount of money offered would be very low anyway, relatively speaking. But the chance to take ownership of a large display in a very public part of the school may motivate some teachers to invest their time, energy and imagination in ways that will surely bring benefit to the whole community. Or perhaps the creative person, who also enjoys directing and managing others, may be the ideal choice for directing the Christmas panto or the leavers' play!

If a person is highly motivated by routine and order, then there is always the timetable to construct, or the new library cataloguing software to install, or the clubs rota, and so on. These are vitally important jobs and the problem-solving and pattern-making therein can even be enjoyable to creatives too! I remember being genuinely motivated by hammering the timetable into shape when the task fell to me as a Deputy Head Academic.

The most successful schools are those in which each member of the team is engaged in work that they find stimulating and motivating, and everyone believes in the vision that the leader has set for the school. There are myriad tasks to go around – we all know that schools are immensely busy places with so much work to be done all through the year. It is better to encourage staff to take on roles that will bring them satisfaction than to coerce them – notwithstanding there are certain tasks that every teacher must do whether they are motivating or not (I'm thinking report writing and examination marking here!).

In my experience, when a teacher loses motivation, they will quickly lose engagement and connection with what they are doing. This can so easily lead to an apathetic approach to school life, doing the minimum required and clocking off as soon as is allowed. I have often seen some teachers make a dash for their cars before all the children have been collected and I can't help but feel sorry for those who clock-watch everyday and pack their bags as the last lesson of the day finishes. 'When will the bell ring, and end this weariness?' as D H Lawrence famously wrote. His poem, 'Last Lesson of the Afternoon', may ring a bell for many of us. Few teachers are immune to the feelings of apathy and despair when faced by Lawrence's 'dross of indifference' sometimes seen in the children. As the poet asks, 'What is the purpose of this teaching of mine and this learning of theirs?'

I have been consumed by this question for much of my career, as many reflective teachers are, perhaps. I have worked with many teachers as a consultant, looking into what exactly keeps them motivated and time and again it comes down to *meaning* and *purpose*. Many of us, including myself, just don't seem able to escape the need for what we are doing during working hours to *make sense* and *have a moral purpose*. The Searcher in James Sale's Motivational Map™ is the motivator that appears most often in schools. Many of us are looking for something to believe in. The phrase, 'to make a difference' probably comes up more than any other in job interviews in education. And for those who are so motivated by purpose and making a difference, keeping the long vision in mind is essential.

Keeping the vision in sight

It is crucial that a school leader has a clear vision and that his or her staff know it, buy into it, and are motivated to turn it into a reality, so that all staff feel they too are making a difference, bringing benefit to others, and their work has purpose and meaning. The vision for the school will be the thing that enables everyone to remain motivated. Involving staff in activities that clearly form part of a school development plan and clearly bring benefit to the children and to the school is so very important – but it's difficult sometimes. Certain tasks – like the report writing and examination marking referred to above – don't seem especially visionary or even purposeful sometimes.

As a headteacher I often struggle to find real purpose behind the kind of assessment data which I am supposed to care deeply about and have to treat with the utmost importance when preparing for a looming Ofsted inspection. It's not that I don't value pupil progress – I know that all children can and should reach their potential, I just don't think the progress children make can be measured exclusively by looking at reading, writing and maths scores. My school development plan was originally named a rapid attainment plan, or RAP for short. Whether you call it a RAP, a development plan or an improvement plan, such a document must feature an outcomes section, in which your data targets are clearly published; but I don't design every element of my plan with the sole purpose of raising levels in literacy and numeracy, however important these aspirations are. I know that improvement, including academic attainment, comes from a holistic approach to learning, encompassing enrichment, pastoral care, moral, spiritual and cultural support. All these things ultimately support the raising of standards because they support the invisible skills and attitudes in the children – and these lead to better habits of learning. The 'rapid attainment' which I know to be so important in my current school will only come, and be sustainable when it does, if we plan for a general improvement in the learning experience for our children. If you want a car to improve its performance you don't just focus on the speedometer.

But the truth remains, if I want my school to stay open we must reach and maintain those all-important standards of attainment. And that means data. But I am not striving to raise academic levels in order to please Ofsted alone! I am, like everyone else in the school, doing it for the children – as Ofsted inspectors themselves would want, I have no doubt. It's why the system was set up, if you look at it from a wider perspective, like from the moon for example (any closer and you will become engulfed in the usual minutiae and feelings of self-doubt that such a system of accountability produces). If we all stared at education from the moon, I think we would all recognise that even the annual submitting of assessment data for reading, writing and maths contributes, ultimately, to improving the life and work opportunities for our children. They need to read and write in order to gain employment, earn money, have a family, acquire a home and so on. And those things *do* motivate all of us in the end. We cannot do much about the goals and expectations placed on our schools by those charged with overseeing us, but we can control the way we respond, especially in the way we internalize those goals and the conversations we have with ourselves about their ultimate purpose.

Staring through a telescope at the things that we find monotonous or without purpose from way up on the lunar surface so that we retain a sense of perspective is not easy. But it's what a school leader does. Having an overview, an ability to step back and not only question the purpose of things, but to *find* purpose in things we do at school is a valuable skill in terms of one's motivation and you don't need to be standing on the moon to have perspective in your job. It is the job of a headteacher to provide that vision, that long view, and remind colleagues of it constantly, so that staff know why we're doing this and where we are headed, ultimately. Making the long view visible for all, and reminding everyone of it, is an essential part of a school leader's job.

Revisiting the school's core values and aims to see how and where one's own role and work fits in is not only useful for one's own motivation, but crucial for the school itself. This is more motivating, I might suggest, than moaning in the staff room come exam time that you don't make children taller by measuring them, or you don't fatten the proverbial pig by weighing him. Of course you don't. But you won't know if he's fatter unless you weigh him, at least sometimes. The pig farmer who refuses to do so may be living in denial, or not especially good at remembering to feed his pigs in the first place.

Viewing one's job in education from a safe distance, allows you to avoid these clichéd arguments. It is essential then that the school leader makes his or her vision explicitly clear, because it is this which allows staff to retain their sense of perspective (see the next chapter).

It is worth noting that the guide to finding motivation at work which I offered in Figure 2 contains only a small number of tasks that may motivate a teacher at school; there are so many others. But note how my list of suggestions for motivational activities in Figure 2 did not include the following, all of which can obscure the long vision for many of us:

- reprimanding children for persistent, silly behaviour in class

- marking books and exam scripts

- ranking children's scores

- handling difficult parents

- teaching an observed lesson

- tidying up after the children

- doing a playground duty in winter

- managing a noisy dining hall

- telling Jason to tuck his shirt in again, and then again, and then again, and it's not even lunchtime yet

Few teachers are motivated by such tasks and they cloud our vision, but they are still necessary in order to achieve the ultimate goals we set ourselves. So it is a case of taking the rough with the smooth, just as it is for the children. Not every task in a school will be motivating for staff, just as not every task for children is motivating. But knowing what does or does not motivate you in the first place is a good place to begin. Taking advantage of opportunities that you know will motivate you may help you to cope with the other tasks that you find less motivating. The key is knowing what drives you in the first place. Fortunately the job of teaching brings so many different tasks, from cognitive behaviour therapist to mathematician, nurse to display artist. There is usually something in the role for everyone.

Keeping children motivated

Just as we, as teachers, find some tasks more motivating, more visionary, than others, the same is true for the children. In Figure 3 below, I offer a similar guide for students at school, which I hope will enable teachers to boost motivational levels and raise engagement in the classroom. It may even help you to reduce absenteeism, since the children will want to come to school if their experiences speak to their intrinsic motivations.

Motivator	Description	Teaching strategies
Searcher	• likes to feel what they are doing is important and has meaning • needs to see value and purpose in tasks • wants to improve things • likes to see the bigger picture • can be disorganised • dislikes routine, prefers variety • insatiably curious	• emphasise the value and benefit in tasks set, both for them and others • provide variety in tasks and formats • allow them to ask questions and brainstorm new ideas/solutions • give extra support with personal organisation and routines • works well with Creators/Spirits • can struggle with Builders/Defenders
Spirit	• needs freedom and opportunity to make independent decisions • a fast thinker, able to see the bigger picture • high levels of energy • prefers to work alone • needs positive feedback • can be disorganised so needs deadlines and limits set	• show them how every action can contribute to the bigger picture • provide constant feedback and focus • structure is important, so break up tasks into individual steps • motivate with positive feedback as much as possible, promoting their decision-making and choices made discuss their long term goals
Creator	• highly motivated by new projects, new problems to solve • enjoys creating new things • copes well with change, dislikes routine, can feel bored quickly • high levels of perseverance • needs to feel the 'play buzz' to be engaged and motivated • responds well to use of colour	• provide problem-solving activities as much as possible • set open-ended activities in which they can feel some ownership • give them time to share creations • provide intellectual stimulation • build time for brainstorming/planning • works well with Searchers and Spirits • can struggle with Defenders

Expert	• highly motivated by learning new things • likes the opportunity to show what they know, teach others • dislikes repetition, prefers to move on to new things quickly • wants to read beyond and around set topics • enjoys sharing knowledge • can appear impatient at times • wants recognition	• provide extension work and guidance for wider reading • provide opportunity to share with the group what they have learned • support if work is routine and repetitive • reward extra efforts and reading • encourage presentations that involve research and training • ensure work is challenging works well most other types
Builder	• driven by need for possessions and material gain • highly motivated by the latest gadgets, including learning tools and equipment in class • works well for reward and material incentives • likes to set clear goals • can be highly competitive	• channel their competitiveness into working hard for group reward • create scenarios in which they role play marketing, advertising, sales • set clear goals and targets and reward when these are met • provide support to guard against jealousy or resentment can struggle with Searchers
Director	• wants to be leading a group • needs some degree of autonomy in their learning/work • motivated by managing others in a team and setting goals • needs constant challenge • wants to see the end goal and will set their own action plan to reach it	• appoint them as group leader whenever possible • establish clearly defined roles • set success criteria and group goals • consider how they can make some decisions themselves • can struggle with Spirits or Friends requires support to see others' contributions and values
Star	• needs to be recognised • likes to be at centre of things • wants to be visibly rewarded • will push themselves to be the best in the group • likes to set themselves goals for what they want to achieve • ambitious and focused	• within reason, ensure their praise and recognition is visible and public • provide responsibility within group work so their role is recognised • establish and follow success criteria • use house points, credits, stars often • manage carefully when working with Stars or Creators

Friend	• needs to feel they belong and are a valued member of team • likes to feel they're being listened to • wants fulfilling relationships • can be very loyal and sociable • needs continuity and proper time to prepare for any change	• always use their name when talking to them to show you are listening • pair up with partners whom they like and trust • encourage them to become mentors or buddies for new pupils • ensure classroom is welcoming and group work is respectful and friendly
Defender	• feels most comfortable when roles and tasks are made clear • prefers routine and can feel unsettled by unplanned change • enjoys working on plans and preparations • can be very loyal and enjoys being part of a team with identifiable roles and duties	• make plans clear, including timescale, learning objectives and expectations • provide personal support to clarify any concerns at the planning stage • take interest in them and their ideas • reward them by highlighting their value within the team/group • can struggle with Creators, Searchers and Spirits who favour new changes

Figure 3: A teacher's guide to raising pupil motivation

Self-motivated children learn better; they show more enthusiasm, more energy and they listen more keenly. The irony is that the various forms of extrinsic motivators available to the teacher, such as the usual stars and house points, may do little for self-motivation in the long term. Working hard, achieving well, trying to be the best one can be – these things are rarely sustained for any significant period by extrinsic rewards and sanctions. Something deeper is required. Finding out what motivates children inside, where their element lies, allows a teacher to find and draw out their natural energies and enthusiasms.

So, can motivation be taught?

Do we need lessons on how to stay motivated? Perhaps. But I suggest that a school's curriculum is already bursting at the seams, and as a consequence so is the timetable. Just like other components of the invisible curriculum on which this series is based, such as character or creativity for example – qualities that make up our 'invisible ink' – motivation may not be best taught and modelled by framing it in a discrete subject called 'Motivation Classes' taught on a Thursday morning, between maths and French. Such a compartmentalising of children's invisible ink will only lead to some staff neglecting to refer to it in other lessons, because it is covered in a separate class. Let's face it, there are many issues and lessons that could, and arguably should, be covered in a cross-curricular way that have now been compartmentalised neatly into weekly PSHE lessons, the responsibility of the PSHE coordinator (like spelling is the responsibility of the English coordinator!). It would seem a pity for motivation to go the same way.

Rather, we need to create the ideal conditions in the classroom in which pupils' self-motivation is fostered. We need to create the right growing conditions. This is what this series is all about. I offer in the next few chapters suggestions on how we can develop motivation in school, by focusing on six key features of the learning environment.

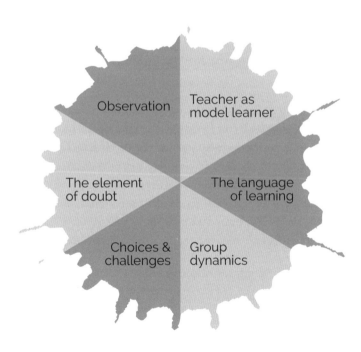

Figure 4: Six key features of the learning environment

3 Teacher as model learner

As with all elements that make up the invisible curriculum, motivation may not be taught in the conventional way, like concepts or skills in the visible curriculum, but it can be passed on to the children through osmosis – that is to say it can be modeled by the teacher for the children to mimic. One cannot coerce a child to be motivated, but one can create the conditions in which they feel disposed to be motivated, and this is what the next few chapters are about.

If you sit next to someone who yawns, the chances are you will yawn too. If that person smiles you will probably smile too, just as if they frown, so will you. If your neighbour is feeling optimistic and energised, you may pick up on some of their energy. Similarly, if the person at the front of the class is greeting a new topic in a motivated and animated way, it is an easier sell to the young buyers than if the teacher is introducing the topic, taught for the seventeenth time perhaps, with a stale and uninspired tone. Children are very perceptive. They will know if the teacher feels uninspired, just as they will know if their teacher is teaching them because it's their job to do so and they won't get paid if they don't. This is contrary to the DfE's Teachers' Standards and I encourage school leaders to hold staff to account when they are not demonstrating consistently 'the positive attitudes, values and behaviour which are expected of pupils' (DfE, 2011: 10). Equally, we can expect teachers to 'maintain good relationships with pupils' (DfE, 2011: 12) and hold them to account when they are not doing so, for the relationship a teacher enjoys with his or her pupils will ultimately have the greatest influence on the learning that happens in their class.

When the teacher enjoys a positive rapport with her students and gains their trust and confidence, those pupils will mimic the attitudes, values and behaviours they see in the teacher. So it is essential that they make a positive contribution to the life of the school – they are, after all, being watched by the children all of the time and their 'invisible influence' will have significant impact whether they like it, or know it, or not. Much of this series is built on this dynamic – the teacher is the model learner in the room, being constantly observed and mimicked by the children. Motivation is no different. The self-motivated teacher will model the kind of positive attitude and energetic approach to learning that we wish to see in the children. It just works that way, it really does. The teacher doesn't just facilitate learning, she shows that learning is exciting and worth doing.

Is it possible to fake motivation? Can we feign interest in a subject? Of course we can. We do it every day as part of our job. How else can a teacher appear motivated to deliver a lesson on adverbs when he or she has been doing so for the last five years, or fifteen years, or thirty? How else can a teacher show enthusiasm for a lesson on fractions other than by delivering a performance in which they are acting as if they were motivated and interested in fractions? It's what we do.

So what does the motivated teacher, being the model learner in the room, actually look like? How do they act? Though it is a component of the invisible curriculum – perhaps even underpinning all other components in this series – motivation is indeed visible in the energetic actions and enthusiastic efforts with which we greet learning objectives in class. Perhaps this is why teaching is such an unusual profession. It requires not only an expert knowledge of the subject being taught, but also a knowledge of how to deliver that subject enthusiastically and in a fashion that excites the interest and curiosity of those listening in class. Teachers who lack this may ultimately struggle to maintain pupils' interest or motivation.

That is not to say the teacher is a children's entertainer. Anyone can do that. Anyone can curry favour with the children and make them feel excited and happy, by saying the right things to them, promising them sweets and making them laugh a lot. Toilet jokes usually work well, or anything to do with bodily functions. We could learn how to make little dogs out of balloons, or learn a magic trick or two. We could make cruel jokes about parents being embarrassing or grandpas farting whilst they're asleep. This is all very entertaining, but it's not what I mean when I talk about enthusing and engaging children. The skill – and the art, because teaching is very much an art form – lies in teaching children at the same time as capturing their interest and imagination and making them feel good. The best lessons are often the ones when the children don't realise they are learning – when learning feels closer to play than to work. I suspect that the executives of modern, creative companies like Google might agree with this.

A teacher is not there just to impart expert knowledge to a child who will then receive it, understand it and be able to recall it on demand in a future examination! What's in it for the child? Why should they learn it? How will it benefit them? They haven't pitched up at school voluntarily. They need to feel a 'play buzz'. They haven't chosen independently to arrange an appointment to see the teacher, like a patient sees a doctor. There is an invisible dynamic going on and it requires the teacher to impart her knowledge with passion, interest and motivation. If the teacher gives an impression that the lesson content is interesting to her, and worth knowing, then the child may decide to show interest too. If she doesn't, then neither will he. Teachers who grasp this early on in their career will go on to enjoy great success and perhaps even enjoyment in the job. The thing which motivates most teachers – and the reason for going into the profession in the first place – is often seeing children learn well and make progress. If feigning interest in lessons will ultimately lead to this end goal then surely it is worth doing. Rather than 'feigning interest', perhaps we should say 'delivering an engaging performance' instead.

A self-motivated learner will learn not because they are coerced into learning through sanctions, or because of the promise of extrinsic rewards, but because they are genuinely interested in what they are doing and want to learn more. Giving the impression that one is self-motivated as a teacher will help to bring this about. It's an osmotic process.

Inspiring and motivating pupils is something which features in the DfE's teachers standards too (not that this may motivate you necessarily, of course!). 'A teacher must set high expectations which inspire, motivate and challenge pupils' (DfE, 2011: 10).

In my experience, a teacher will show enthusiasm and motivation at work when he or she believes that they are part of something bigger, something special, and that their efforts to teach pupils effectively will contribute to this wider vision. There is nothing quite so motivating as feeling that we are helping to build something special and we are part of it too. When the direction of travel is upwards, and our own contributions can be seen as directly affecting this trajectory, then we will feel even more motivated. And so the momentum grows. This is why school improvement plans are so important and why they need to speak to every member of staff in the school.

The motivated teacher

A school's core values are of great importance here. The teacher needs to embody them, rather than point to them on a wall. And the same is true of motivation.

So what does a self-motivated teacher look like? How do they function in class and around the school?

Without wishing to state the obvious, a smile goes a long way. This can be very motivating for children. If I think back to my own school days, the teachers for whom I felt the most motivated to work were the ones who smiled at me. They smiled at everyone. They radiated warmth and positivity, even on rainy Mondays. It is astonishing how far a smile goes. The teacher who shows a sunny disposition will always carry the children with them; but the teacher who frowns and glares in the classroom and moans and groans in the staff room will ignite no fires in those they meet, they will only extinguish them.

In *Essential Motivation in the Classroom* (2002), Ian Gilbert reminds us that reacting to a smile runs deep within us all.

> One of the very first images we focus on is the smiling face of our mother. That image of two eyes and a smiley face stays with us, deep down in our psyche. When someone smiles at us, an automatic smile response is triggered whether we like it or not. Something fires that distant memory and we smile back, we start to feel good whether we like it – or even notice it – or not. I am aware that there are some teachers who have managed to suppress their automatic smile response through years of abuse and dubious INSET. Even so, research found that the muscles around our mouth do react, albeit imperceptibly, when someone smiles at us. In other words, you can turn a class around with a smile. (Gilbert, 2002: 139)

This is a picture that many of us may recognise. To smile at a class is not to ignore errant behaviour or pretend everything is fine when it may not be. Tough love means showing warmth and affection even when it feels like the last thing we want to do. When all we want to do is frown and reprimand, a smile can often have the results we ultimately want, over time. And as model learner, a sunny disposition will help us encourage the children to present a positive attitude both to the learning and to themselves as learners. Of course, too often in education the pendulum swings from one extreme to another, polarized stances are taken and anyone who suggests we should smile more in class will immediately be interpreted by others as a person who is anti-reprimanding or anti-discipline. But once again, it's not either/or, it is *and*. Good teachers, like good parents, know that far from being mutually exclusive, love and discipline are necessary partners for bringing up children. This is what I mean by robust love.

My favourite phrase at the moment, and one which I use regularly in staff meetings because it is so apposite in my current workplace, is 'robust optimism'. I like to think that my optimism for my school and its exciting future is robust enough to withstand bad news whenever it comes (as it usually does every day, in one form or another). My robust optimism means I am impervious to cynicism. I won't accept it in my school, either in the lesson or in the staff room. I believe that the ability to maintain a smile is a prerequisite for the job. The old adage 'don't smile until Christmas' is nonsense, surely, and will do precious little to create a shared excitement about learning. Enthusiasm is infectious, after all. Only the most hardened cynics in the staff room will not be infected by a positive disposition and this, usually, leads to them isolating themselves in the end.

Another trait of the self-motivated teacher is that they will project high expectations for themselves and for others. They have clear aspirations and set high goals. They do not settle for mediocrity, but always see the potential for better things, better results. Embodying a growth mindset, the self-motivated teacher believes anything is possible with hard work and enthusiasm. Again, such an attitude may be tiresome for cynics but it is essential in moving the learning on and encouraging children to raise their chins and aim high, especially in rural village schools set in idyllic Suffolk countryside, as mine is. A perceived lack of ambition in such places can be 'Suffolkating' as I once heard it described. Many of my pupils' parents were themselves educated at my current school and many of their grandparents too. They are a loyal and loving community, in which the school is a well-respected hub of the village. But having clear aspirations and high expectations for the children need not be unsettling for such a community rooted by a strong sense of place and tradition. Everyone wants their child to have an ambitious, self-motivated teacher, no matter where they live. Children are entitled to be the subject of high aspiration wherever they come from.

In her book, *Make School Better*, Professor Sonia Blandford writes about the importance of having high aspirations and expectations:

> Every parent and carer wants the best for their children, but we can all unintentionally lower our children's expectations of school and themselves. Perhaps this is because of our own negative experience of school and memory of it. Perhaps because schools don't communicate to parents and carers what is going on and how children are doing in an effective way. (Blandford, 2015: 34)

I share this concern and this is why I have introduced a new school newsletter/review which goes out to parents electronically every month. It is filled with contributions from each teacher, all about the various successes their children have had in class, and beyond. It has lots of exciting pictures of the children learning and playing and succeeding. It is a publication that unashamedly celebrates how talented our children are and how exciting our school is. In so doing, it is helping me to raise the aspirations of our children and the expectations of our parents. You might say we are creating our own pressure which we as teachers must live up to every time. After all, we cannot now produce a magazine that has no achievement in it – we have to up the ante every issue.

A third characteristic of the self-motivated teacher, acting as model learner, is that they are seen to enjoy a challenge! How we embrace challenges when they come along is so important, as teachers. When things become difficult for us – perhaps when we have a our annual dose of flu, or when we simply have too many books to mark, or when we accompany the children on the obligatory sponsored run – the children will be watching us, studying our every move, mimicking how we are, what we say and what we do. We are model learners whether we like it or not and the resilience and robust optimism we display, especially in difficult times, will be picked up and learned by the children. The moment we show defeat or resignation, the moment we show a shrug or express a huff and a tut, we are indirectly robbing the children of their own motivation – giving them licence to show apathy and defeatism.

As model learners we must teach the children that challenges are good for us, they are exciting. It is good to be in the 'learning pit' – to be in the place when we feel challenged and need to scratch our heads and work out what to do next. This is the exciting part, the challenge. And it feels all the more exciting when we conquer the challenge and climb out of the learning pit a better, wiser person for it. The trick is encouraging children to climb into the learning pit in the first place, rather than remaining on solid land which is familiar and comfortable for them. As the model learner in the room we need to show that it's okay to be stuck, to be not sure or to be confused about what to do next. That is when real learning happens, provided we have a positive, 'can-do' attitude.

An ability to combat negative thoughts is also crucial for the self-motivated, model learner. As teachers we are cognitive behaviour therapists, after all, tackling the children's negative views of themselves and of their own abilities. We spend much of our working lives reinforcing, inspiring, chivvying and motivating. The motivated teacher won't tolerate defeatism or pessimism in children; neither will they welcome it in the staff room. We always look to encourage children to see themselves in a positive light, as able doers rather than passive observers. We want them to plunge in and join the team, safe in the knowledge that they are indeed 'good enough' to participate. Having a poor image of oneself is such a problem for many school children and it can lead to terrible consequences of self-harming and worse, as we read about in the media all too often. Maintaining a positive view of oneself and one's own ability is perhaps the single most important thing for a child in school, especially when they hit adolescence and the paranoia and low self-esteem that it can often bring.

Most of us have a little voice in our head telling us we cannot do it, we're not good enough, others are better than us. In his celebrated book, *The Chimp Paradox*, Steve Peters reminds us that not only do we have a Chimp inside of us, and a Human and a Computer, we have Gremlins too. One such Gremlin could well be a belief that we are not as good as other people. Peters offers a story which I for one find all too familiar:

Let's say you are waiting in a queue to buy a cup of coffee

and someone pushes in front of you. You, the Human, may want to politely say, 'Excuse me, there is a queue,' and your Chimp might want to say the same thing but in a much more aggressive manner! However, before either of you get a chance to speak, you and the Chimp look into the Computer. Here you will see the Gremlin who says, 'You are not as good as other people.' This is the reference for the Human and the Chimp to act on. So this Gremlin prevents you from speaking because you feel you do not have the right or you fear the person's response. (Peters, 2012: 91)

The self-motivated, self-confident teacher is able to silence this Gremlin (Peters might say he has replaced the Gremlin with an Autopilot – a learned response that counters the negative thought).

The word 'autopilot' seems especially apt for us teachers. There have been moments when I have cruised on autopilot, wearing a resilient grin like a shield, often when other adults outside the profession might question why I accepted this or ignored that or didn't dish out some Victorian punishment but chose to meet difficult behaviour with a patient and understanding smile. (If only I could do the same at home, my wife would cry if she read this).

But resilience and patience will win in the end, always. The teacher, as model learner, needs self-confidence and positive thinking at all times. He or she does not possess a reverse gear, only forward gears – always moving on, never dwelling on past mistakes and failures, but showing resilience to keep going and trying to be better next time. 'It's all good' is another phrase I use around the corridors and classrooms of my school and, though I'm sure it attracts much teasing from my colleagues, it reinforces the message that the school's future, and the future of all the children within it, continues to look promising. And so it is. If we as model learners believe it's all good, then it generally is.

But negative thinking cannot be swept so easily under the carpet or scrunched up and put in the bin simply by having a robustly optimistic approach! It's deeper than that. It may be that negative thinking is a design fault within us all. Think about it. Whenever we hear some criticism, no matter how small, we clutch onto it and save it for later when we will chide ourselves for being so rubbish. We may have had a day filled to the brim with good things, glowing praise and acclaim from colleagues and parents, but one piece of criticism and the part of us that wallows in self-pity will feast on it for twenty-four long hours. It is a constant battle between the voice inside that thinks we can and the voice that thinks we can't. Sadly, the former requires constant reassurance, while the latter is quite happy to go on believing we're rubbish without any real evidence to suggest this is true! Even the smallest crumb of criticism will be enough to keep that voice going.

So responding to criticism robustly and optimistically is an important skill for the self-motivated, model learner. Taking comments on board and not allowing them to cloud our overall judgement of ourselves and our ability is important and children need to learn how to do this. Most of us are fragile and we frown at the idea of being so resilient that we can take criticism lightly – this seems arrogant. Modesty and a self-deprecating nature are quite British traits, aren't they; but as charming as they are, children may miss the subtleties here. Modesty is important, of course, but we can all too easily give children the impression it's okay to mock ourselves and never good form to be boastful about our own abilities. It's such a minefield isn't it! (Or perhaps a mindfield?)

In Key Stage 1, the traditional model of the 'show and tell' works wonders. 'Weekend news' is welcome in the classroom too. It seems a pity that this often peters out once the children rise up through the school. Things which the children have achieved in their own lives outside school are very, very important and they must receive airtime in school. Every child needs that special moment when they can show what they've done or experienced, where they've been, what they have achieved. This is not boastful; it is providing that all-important reassurance to the inner voice that we *are* good enough, we *can* achieve great things and we can go on to achieve even more.

As model learners, we too can be proud of what we have achieved, rather than self-deprecating. When we show pride in our work and in our appearance we project an image that we care about ourselves, perhaps we even like ourselves? We show that we have self-respect. It is often saddening when we see a teacher who is so snowed under with work, so consumed by assessment and marking and report writing, that they begin to show less concern for their appearance and their health. It is a story so familiar to us all – we begin the term with a sense of optimism and in good health and by Christmas we have become so tired, so overworked and so overwhelmed that we are a shadow of our former selves. Do we really think the children haven't noticed this decline? They may be the most observant, attentive people in our lives. They *notice* things about us. And above all, they notice when we are feeling low about ourselves. This gives them licence to feel low about their own selves, and so the spiral of negative thinking and low self-esteem continues. Though it is a mantle that weighs heavy sometimes, we are beacons of hope and optimism in our classrooms.

And they say teachers are just in it for the holidays! Teaching is like being on a submarine. We dive in late August and we don't resurface until a few days before Christmas, regardless of what those outside the profession may think! Our half-term holidays disappear in a melee of marking, refreshing displays and poring over scripts for the Christmas pantomime. No wonder it is difficult to maintain a healthy body and mind! But positive thinking, self-respect and a smile can conquer just about problem that a school can throw at you. Robust optimism will always win (provided it is accompanied by a willingness to tackle problems head on and lots of hard work, of course!).

Finding opportunities at work to boost your motivation

In Figure 2 above I suggested some ways of boosting your motivation at work, depending on what your intrinsic motivators are. This is extremely important when viewing the teacher as model learner. Once you have identified the tasks you find most motivating at work then you can set about focusing on them – not exclusively, of course, (you would not last long in your job if you only did these tasks) but you can manage your time efficiently so that you can devote some time each week to motivational activity. It may be appropriate that you can assemble a team of students to assist you in these endeavours, such as constructing elaborate displays, creating a tidy and well-organised classroom, or managing the school resources cupboard. In the case of something like directing school productions or conducting a school choir, clearly you will need the help of students anyway! If the children can see you 'in your element' then they will mimic the character traits and attitudes you show at the time.

In the very best schools, the teachers are motivated and energised, and their influence spreads to the children. The staff are in the right roles, doing the right things for them, things that motivate them and get them out of bed in the morning. They want to learn more in their own field and reflect on their practice constantly to see how they can improve. There is a collegiate feel, a sense that together they are building something special. Conversely, the worst schools are populated by people who, for whatever reason, lack the drive and ambition to set high aspirations either for themselves or for others, and many may be doing the job for the money only. They may feel that they have learned enough to be able to do the job and there is no need to learn any more. Some colleagues may not have attended a CPD course for several years and they may not see the need to. If we are model learners for the students, it is essential that we can show we too are learning year on year, and showing evidence of our own professional development. It is a pity that in these times of financial constraints, staff training budgets can often be the first to be cut. But there are still many opportunities in house for sharing knowledge and inspiring each other to reflect on their own pedagogy and practice. Since I began at my current school I have been constantly promoting the idea of peer-to-peer coaching and the evidence we are collecting from staff suggests that this is already leading to a more reflective and mindful approach to our teaching. And it doesn't cost any extra money, only cover time, which like most school leaders I am always happy to provide if I can.

We are fortunate that schools have so many different types of tasks within them, from creating displays and directing school plays to stock taking and organising resources cupboards! There should be something for everyone, perhaps in addition to what their job description actually says. The trick is knowing one's staff well enough to know which opportunities you can present to them in order to facilitate most satisfaction for them and thus bring most benefit for the school community.

Whether we take up those opportunities depends very much on our state of mind at work – whether we choose to be optimistic or pessimistic, whether we choose a growth mindset or a defeatist one.

Can you choose to be motivated?

I conducted an experiment the other day. It was a rainy Saturday. Typically, the previous few days had been bathed in glorious autumnal sunshine and yet I had not set a foot outside due to being snowed under with paperwork in my office at school. I had been looking forward to a sunny stroll and was, consequently, feeling glum.

I was feeling tired too – the week at school had been relentlessly difficult (very much the challenge I need in my life, but one can have too much of a prescribed medicine, you understand). I was, it must be said, feeling bereft of any motivation at all that morning.

I gazed out over the soggy fields and watched the mist rolling in, felt the gloom rising. My wife had delicately suggested to the children that Daddy was tired and needed a few minutes' peace to finish his cup of tea.

And then I decided to try my experiment. I told myself I was happy and highly motivated.

Sounds nonsense doesn't it? Like something off a page from a self-help guide on being 'the best you'.

I had nothing especially to be excited and motivated about, but on the other hand I had nothing to be depressed and demotivated about either. I was just tired! In the grand scheme of things, how dare I feel glum!?

So inside my mind I flicked the switch that was firmly on the sad side and moved it to the happy side again. I faked it. I faked my motivation and my enthusiasm. Optimism and pessimism are, after all, places you simply choose to live in, and that morning I made a deliberate choice to live in optimism.

The astonishing thing is, it worked.

I am no psychologist, neurologist or psychiatrist. I have no experience in the actual ways my brain is hard wired, but I do have forty-four years' experience of *me*. And I know how I function, or how I often don't function on a Saturday morning.

The day was one of the most prolific and enjoyable days I have had in a long time. And all because I had flicked the switch across and faked a highly motivated state. I chose to have a positive mindset.

I don't think you can do this every day. But it served as an effective 'jump start' to my flat battery that morning.

I have often said in previous titles in this series that *we* are in control of *ourselves*.

We cannot control what others say, what they do, and we certainly cannot control the weather; but we *can* control the way we respond to these influences. Of that there is no doubt. As model learners in the classroom, we can fake our motivation, fake our enthusiasm and interest, especially in a topic that we have taught for many years before!

In his excellent book, *The 7 Habits of Highly Effective Teenagers*, Sean Covey extends the advice given by his world-famous father, Stephen Covey, to a teenage audience. He explains this element of self-control very succinctly:

> The fact is, we can't control everything that happens to us. We can't control the colour of our skin, who will win the FA Cup, where we are born, who our parents are or how others might treat us. But there is one thing we can control: *how we respond to what happens to us.* (Covey, 1999: 54)

Covey asks us to imagine two concentric circles, the inner circle is our circle of control: 'It includes things we have control over, such as ourselves, our attitudes, our choices, our response to whatever happens to us.' Surrounding this circle is the circle of no control, which includes all the myriad things we have no control over.

Having robust optimism and robust motivation, for me, means carefully controlling the way we respond to circumstances. It means retaining our motivation even when it seems there is nothing to motivate us – and sometimes in the face of circumstances that may otherwise seem demotivating. No one can physically or chemically make us feel sad or demotivated. Only we can do that. And only we can make ourselves motivated or contented.

Leadership is about showing this kind of energy and optimism when situations seem anything but energising or optimistic. Good leaders, and good model learners, have a reserve tank they can dip into when necessary. There will undoubtedly be times in the future that will refill our tanks again – times when we genuinely feel motivated and contented and we are not faking it! But for those moments when we feel down, we can flick the switch across and fake it.

Try it. But don't try it every day. If you feel it is necessary to fake it every day then perhaps you are in the wrong role or the wrong setting, perhaps even the wrong profession. We must have those moments that rejuvenate us and refill our 'invisible ink'. But we can last on reserve for a little while, I'm certain. We can choose to be optimistic.

The blame game

As model learner, feeling empowered and in control of our own responses and therefore our own learning is essential. In recognising that we are in control of the way we respond to circumstances and people around us we can avoid the destructive damage of the 'blame game' – a habit many of us can so easily fall into, where we see ourselves only as victims. Schools need to have a no-excuses culture. It is often tempting to blame our own poor practice or our demotivation on a lack of support from colleagues, at best, or because of the destructive interfering of others, at worst. We find actions and circumstances that lie very much outside Covey's 'inner circle of control' and we blame them for our own mistakes or lack of progress. We may actually blame circumstances that lie beyond our control for the things that we are in control of but have just not done anything about. Are we not influencing the children when we project such resignation? Are we not encouraging them to develop that corrosive condition we call 'learned helplessness'?

For example, we might blame the actions or words of others in the staff room for our own demotivated and negative attitude to work. But this is to mix two very distinct circles: the actions of others lie beyond our control (in Covey's outer circle), but when it comes to our own attitude, this is very much within our control – in fact it cannot be controlled by anyone else, so we cannot blame others if we are feeling negative.

From a learner's point of view, this has relevance. If you think about it, the actions, and particularly the successes, of a child in class will often have an impact on the attitude and motivation of the child sitting next to her. If you want to watch a child's self-motivation and confidence plummet, praise the child sitting next to her for some outstanding work or a positive attitude to learning. Your comments will ricochet around the room, and have particular impact on those in proximity.

How many times have we done this, albeit unknowingly? How many times have you offered some warm words of encouragement to a child, but have not said the same words of encouragement to the other children sharing the same table? It would be preposterous to say the same thing to all children – this would devalue the currency of just about anything you say. But just after we have praised someone on an excellent piece of work, we may turn and miss the look of defeat in the child's neighbour, who feels deflated and worthless by comparison. But tell all children they've done an excellent piece of work and they know you're lying. It's so very difficult!

As model learners, we can emphasise the importance of PBs – personal bests. Progress must be relative not to what the child next to you has done, but to what you did before, what you have shown you are capable of in the past. It is possible to stay motivated in class if we focus on setting ourselves small, manageable targets every lesson and then achieving them – regardless of what others' targets are.

None of us is without flaws; few of us hit the bull's eye every time. As model learner it is worth pointing out what you struggle at – perhaps it is handwriting on the board, or time management or, in my own case, organisational skills and general tidiness. Explain to the class that you are setting yourself a target to write more neatly this week, and that you will give yourself a treat if you can achieve this! You may wish to stress that this target has no connection to others, it is not dependent on others succeeding or failing – only on you, because it is something only you can control. The targets you set are not related to anyone else, and it should not matter if others are already writing neatly! This has nothing to do with your own personal target.

Showing resilience and optimism when receiving criticism is something I have talked a lot about in this series already, and especially in *Teaching for Character*, but from a motivation point of view, equally important is showing resilience and optimism when others near you are praised!

When others in the staff room, or in your own life, receive acclaim and admiration for what they have achieved, this should not in any way affect your own self-motivation and optimism, but sadly it often does. And I think children are no different to this. They may find it even harder to cope with than we adults do.

It's back to those PBs again; setting SMART goals that are bespoke and achievable will help to maintain children's individual motivation levels. Then, when they achieve a personal goal, you can appeal directly to their self-motivation and self-worth. Meeting individual, personal targets also helps to emphasise to a pupil that *they* are in control of *them*.

Easier said than done, perhaps. But you can begin by setting yourself personal goals each week, perhaps each day. Your own self-worth and your self-motivation will increase immeasurably when you start achieving those goals and, as model learner, this can only mean good news for the pupils who are mimicking you.

Having something to believe in

The model learner, like all learners in the room, will be motivated to do their best if they think it is worth it – if they can see a vision of something better and then recognise how their efforts *will* take them to this better place. So expectations need to be high. As teachers we need to present children constantly with a vision of how good they are going to be, how much we believe in them and how special their work will become, if they invest the time and effort. We need to show them that it definitely *is* worth trying.

In my experience of school leadership, one of the most significant influences on staff work rate and attitude to school is if they think the school as a whole is really going somewhere. The vision of the future – of an outstanding school filled with independently learning, deep thinking, well-rounded children – is a supremely important picture that needs to be emphasised and revisited many times in the course of a term. And the same is true for children; independent projects, and collaborative ones too, may take some time to complete but will ultimately be the talk of the school and worthy of much acclaim, not to mention personal satisfaction. As model learners, we can continually show our excitement and enthusiasm for what is to come – we know the final outcome will be impressive and we know this because we are all going to work hard to achieve it. The moment we lose sight of the vision, that is when motivation will decrease.

From a teaching point of view, this means that Learning Objectives, or Learning Intentions, or whatever you currently call them, need to paint a positive vision of the future. Rather than taking them straight from the syllabus (*eg* to use speech marks accurately to denote direct speech/to multiply two digit numbers together) we can re-word them to create that vision of a better future, better learner, higher ability. These need to be empowering, using phrases like 'You will be able to…' and 'You will be better at…'. This will help to maintain motivation during the journey.

4 The language of learning

In all seven titles in this series, I will consider how the language of learning impacts on the invisible curriculum. The terminology we use to monitor, assess and report on the children's character development, creativity and curiosity, for example, can itself shape the very results we see. And motivation is no exception either. We can and we should talk to children in ways that are positive and encouraging at all times, but when we talk to them in the language of their intrinsic motivators too, then communication becomes even more effective.

The first hurdle to overcome is the word 'motivational' itself. As I mentioned in Chapter 1, we are dealing with something that is invisible here and something that for many belongs in a handbook written by and for personal trainers and life coaches, or perhaps it's a word we associate with muscular men selling life-changing DVDs on shopping channels. Look good and you'll feel good. Put on a tracksuit, pump yourself up and you'll feel like a new person. Motivate, motivate, motivate. Come on! Do that squat thrust, finish those exercises, only faster this time. There's nothing stopping you. You *can* do it. Say it with me, 'I *can* do it!'

You get the picture. But where and how and why does the word *motivational* fit into my life? I'm too busy to put on a tracksuit, please. And I stopped watching Bob the Builder a lifetime ago.

Like so many other aspects of learning upon which this series is based, motivation is invisible and therefore difficult for a busy teacher or school leader to place at the top of their priorities list; and the connotations we associate with the word *motivational* don't exactly help.

The Oxford English Dictionary defines 'motivation' as either 'a motive' or 'enthusiasm'. To motivate someone is to provide them with a motive or to stimulate their interest in something.

Having a motive is to have a reason for doing something.

None of these definitions conjure up the same images of fitness instructors or life coaches as the word 'motivational' does. I feel less cynical, less sceptical of the word *motive*. Of course we all need a reason for doing something. What is intriguing is when learners find those reasons from within themselves – they are self-motivated. The reasons they have for working hard and making progress are not linked to extrinsic rewards; rather they are for personal satisfaction, a sense of accomplishment, to satisfy their curiosity, to give vent to their creativity, to express an idea, to articulate an opinion or just simply to have fun.

These are the phrases that we can concern ourselves with as teachers. They are words which we can use when reporting on the children's learning behaviours. When we say something is motivational, we mean it pricks our curiosity or engages our attention, or prompts our enthusiasm.

It's back to those learning objectives again; we need to sell the lesson to the pupils in ways that will do just that – fill them with enthusiasm and prick their curiosity.

Such language may help us to refer to motivation in ways that sound less bound up with motivational management speak and more grounded in the reality of the classroom and the learning experience.

But what about reporting on motivation? What terms are most effective here? How can we encapsulate a child's motivation levels in a written report? How can we evidence their self-motivation?

I suggest we focus on the learning behaviour that is shown in class; this will give us the evidence we need.

Motivation and learning behaviours

The self-motivated child will usually display some of the following learning behaviours, all of which provide actual evidence that can be referred to in a school report:

● asking questions

- engaging in discussions
- working well independently
- taking pride in their work
- volunteering to assist the teacher
- staying on after the lesson has finished to complete some work
- showing evidence of extra research at home
- engaging in discussions with the teacher at break times and lunch times
- being punctual for lessons
- having the right equipment at the right time
- taking pride in their appearance
- showing interest and enthusiasm in lessons
- responding proactively to marking and feedback
- working well as part of a team

In Chapter 8, I will refer to some of these as learning habits that can be used to monitor children's motivation levels. The student who lacks self-motivation, conversely, may display some of the following characteristics and behaviours:

- not working unless directly told to do so
- questioning the purpose of tasks given
- leaving assignments unfinished
- ignoring feedback
- unwilling to participate fully in class discussions
- rarely answering, or asking, questions
- lacking enthusiasm or interest in the lesson
- unwilling to work well as part of a team, unless told to

These behaviour descriptors, good or bad, give us a repertoire of phrases to use when we report on the children's motivation levels. And they enable us to see the significant impact which motivation, or lack of it, will have on the quality and quantity of learning which takes place in class, ultimately impacting on pupils' progress. In this way we see that though motivation itself may be invisible and lies deep within the gut, its effects are visible indeed. If we are to make a judgement about a student's motivation levels, we need to show evidence, and this comes through observing their learning habits and behaviours.

In book one, *Teaching for Character*, I referred to a parents' evening I attended for one of my children. In the book I mentioned that in answer to my question, 'How has my son been performing this term?' his teacher offered me a list of grades. I stated that these were the *results* of his performance, not his performance. What I wanted was a commentary on his learning behaviour in class – and although this anecdote was referenced in the context of my son's character development, the same is true of his motivation too. I want to know if my son is engaging in discussions, asking questions, taking pride in his work, showing interest, and so on. I wanted to know if he is self-motivated.

As teachers I believe we need a script with which to report on these important learning habits. Far from being invisible or an afterthought, motivation is at the heart of it all, and it must be commented upon.

Predictably, so many of my son's school reports comprise sentences that usually begin with the words, 'This term Henry has been studying…' Read past these and you will usually find references to Henry's attainment levels in response to tasks set and tests sat – and these are often described in percentages or grades. But the subtext that I am most interested in, the parts which often have to be gleaned through inference and deduction alone, are precisely these learning behaviours (see Chapter 8 for more on observing and reporting on motivation).

I wonder how much of our marking and feedback is focused on the child's ability, or inability, to understand, retain, process, apply, calculate or explain? These are important learning skills but they are not learning *behaviours*. The self-motivated learner may be able to demonstrate such learning skills, but only, I would suggest, because they have developed good learning behaviours. And they have done that because they are motivated to do so, intrinsically. They have a motive for learning.

And the language we use as part of the teaching and learning discourse will help them to feel self-motivated. Just as the children's motivation is significantly affected by being witness to our own enthusiasm and optimism as model learners, so too will their motivation be increased by our choice of words when feeding back to them on their learning and achievements.

The language of motivation

In previous titles in this series I have emphasised the importance of building a sense of ownership for the pupils – phrasing our language in ways that remind them it is *their* work, *their* behaviour and *their* choices made. This will increase their self-motivation. An *aide-mémoire* I have often used when planning lessons is:

MORE learning: **M**otivation through **O**wnership, **R**esponse, **E**valuation.

It is an old adage that for many children much of the work they do in school and for homework is not really *theirs*. After all, it is the teacher who sets it, the teacher who marks it and the teacher who reviews it. It is often only the teacher who knows where and how the work fits into the medium-term plan and why it is being done at all. So children may consider that for much of the time the efforts they invest in their work are, ultimately, for someone else. This I would argue can be demotivating and may result in the usual cycle of working for extrinsic rewards and sanctions.

By offering the following comments, we can help to emphasise that the child is in control of their learning and of their actions – so therefore they can claim the credit for it, and a sense of accomplishment:

- I like the way you did that!
- I like your choice of words here.
- Your choice of sentence here is impressive.
- Your work is so neatly presented today!
- I like the way you have worked that out.
- Your use of colour here is superb.
- Your use of shading here is excellent.
- Your decision to begin your story in this way is really good.
- Your decision to set it out like that is excellent.

The list is endless. Each time, our feedback is underlining the fact that the child has made the right choice and showed an investment in the work and in themselves as learners.

These comments are different from just plain compliments; they are focused on specific tasks the children have done well and the use of 'your' and 'you' is reinforcing the idea that the work is theirs, not yours. Compliments like 'Aren't you clever!' are about as useful as saying 'Aren't you tall!'. We need a growth mindset rather than a fixed one and we need to avoid putting pressure on the children next time around by saying that they are really creative, or really talented! We can separate the learning behaviours and learning skills shown from the actual learner. This allows them to move on and upwards or to the side or somewhere completely different next time, without needing to live up to a reputation, albeit a positive one. It's a strange dynamic but I've often found that when someone calls me 'very creative' I feel less motivation to create something else. It is pressure. But if they tell me that a picture I have drawn or a poem I have written is enjoyable or interesting or imaginative then I feel spurred on to do it again. The difference here is I am being taken out of the picture, it is the creation I have produced that is in the spotlight and I feel no pressure to live up to a reputation. Besides, if someone says I am very creative, does this mean I have reached my goal and cannot aspire to it anymore? I wasn't painting or writing in order to be seen as creative, I was doing it because I needed to express a thought or a mood or an idea. It wasn't about me, it was about the piece. I'm sure professional artists struggle when they receive praise – I assume they have to build a shield around themselves, protecting them from the complacency of finding out you're really, really good at what you do. The struggle is over.

But each new piece of work is a fresh start. The children must feel that they can surprise us every time, and surprise themselves too. The last thing we should say is 'I knew you could do it!' or 'You've done it again!' no matter how tempting or well-intentioned such phrases are. But once they have written or made something impressive, we can remind the children that they did it, they invested in themselves and look at the results! We can do this without giving them the mantle of being creative or being clever. Such nomenclature may ultimately be demotivating, ironically.

Not all children feel motivated to learn just so that they can please you, and receive glowing praise. Rather, they need to feel that all-important sense of accomplishment and sense of ownership. If they can make the right choices now, they can do so again. It *is* worth trying.

Have you noticed that when you do tell a child they are very creative or talented or clever they often shy away from the praise? They will sometimes shrug and say it was nothing or quickly point out a flaw in what they have created. I don't believe this is false modesty. I believe they don't want to be in the limelight for what they have done – this may not have the reason why they did it in the first place. They *enjoyed the challenge, the risks along the way*. Something kept them engaged and trying their best – it was their self-motivation.

Optimism about children's potential is crucial if we are to maintain their self-motivation in learning. And if we are to acknowledge the untapped potential of our pupils then we must make many of our tasks sufficiently open-ended to allow for that element of surprise, that risk – to allow for them to surprise us and themselves with what they have created. Perhaps this is why I have such a problem with 'success criteria'. It has become very fashionable in school to set a learning objective and then set success criteria for how to achieve that learning objective. Often the learning objective and the success criteria are printed onto little sheets and stuck into books before the children have put pen to paper.

I have seen some such sheets that contain a row of three faces, a smiley one, an expressionless one and a sad one. The idea, I think, is for the child to colour in the smiley face if they have 'got it', the expressionless one if they're not quite sure and the sad one if they haven't a clue. I have seen this method adopted in schools and I have often asked the children what this sheet is for during learning walks I have conducted. A significant number of children tell me, 'I coloured in the sad face because I got it wrong and that makes the teacher sad.'

Can you imagine?

But involving the child in his or her learning is, of course, a worthwhile teaching strategy. Assessment-for-learning, as it is often called, can be very effective, provided the criteria is clear and the ways in which children are to assess their own efforts cannot be misconstrued!

But should we be laying down the success criteria for everything they do? Are we in danger of reducing their motivation if we mark out the ground first? Where's the surprise?

We believe we are scaffolding learning, facilitating the children's better understanding of what is expected of them, how they are going to achieve it and how they will know when they've succeeded. But are we not in danger here of laying down the perimeters too much? Are we not limiting the children's potential, ultimately, by setting the boundaries and the outcomes in such granular detail?

For me at least, when I plan so meticulously, setting out what I want to achieve, and exactly how I'm going to get there, I feel in my mind I've already accomplished it. I can envision with great clarity the finished product and I know that this is only going to reduce my intrinsic motivation to start the task. There's no surprise, only disappointment if it didn't live up to expectations. I've already imagined myself finishing the job in my head before I've started it. Perhaps this is why I rarely plan! I find the more detailed the success criteria, the less the surprise at the other end and the less the motivation to begin the quest! I can't imagine how worse it must be when someone else has had a hand in setting the success criteria for me. Can you imagine someone else telling you to write a story and setting out some success criteria so that you know if the story is any good once it's written?

I have experienced performance management appraisals, like all of us have, and I'm not sure I have ever been truly motivated by the success criteria of my new objectives each time. It seems like I am going through the motions, following the routine, in order to meet expectations. How motivating is that, really? Of course, as a headteacher I know it is essential to be given targets and to be able to show how I am working towards them – it doesn't help my motivation particularly, but it has to be done, of course.

I appreciate that children need to know what is expected of them. And some children need to know this all of the time. Good assessment-for-learning pedagogy tells us that we empower children when we equip them with the knowledge and understanding of success criteria and how they personally are meeting those targets along the way. But I still feel that we rob students of their intrinsic motivation to create, surprise and produce something special when the finished product is what we hoped and expected it would be – it matches the success criteria that we had already laid down for them, so how is it going to surprise us, or them?

On the other hand, we cannot simply provide no help along the way – children need guidance and handy hints and tips; they need to know where they are, where they need to get to and how to get there. But must we call it *success criteria*?

I wonder if in terms of language we could remove the word 'success' altogether. We know that if the children follow these steps or meet these targets along the way that they will ultimately be 'successful' (*ie* they will meet our expectations of them), but do we need to flag it up in those terms? Why *success criteria*? Why *learning objective* or *learning intention*? I don't believe any of these words, with the exception of 'learning' perhaps, are especially motivational for a child. Intention? Objective? I can hear a robotic voice in my head monotonously chanting 'must meet objective, must meet objective...'

It is a difficult conundrum. On the one hand, we want to lay out before the children the route to succeeding; and we want them to take charge of their learning along the way, checking against the success criteria to see if they are on the right path. But on the other hand, we want to set them challenges that carry a degree of surprise, a sense of autonomy and decision-making. So that, ultimately, what we get is a synthesis of their ideas and ours, an amalgam of exemplar work that matches the criteria *and* demonstrates some originality.

Rather than 'success criteria' I prefer 'handy hints' or 'route map'. The latter especially suggests the student is embarking on a journey somewhere – it gives a feeling of motion, of adventure even. There is still a sense of a set destination, of course, but perhaps a route map is more empowering for the traveller than a series of detailed directions. Remember, the ultimate purpose of this is to keep the learner motivated to push on and do their best.

5 Group dynamics

Some children are motivated by being part of a team; to use Turner and Sale's terminology, their top motivation is 'Friend' and they are motivated by enjoying positive relationships with others, working together and relying on one another. For others though, being part of a team may not be motivating at all and emphasising the team spirit will do little for their intrinsic motivation to work hard and do their best.

As with any aspect of teaching, it is about knowing the students well enough to know which are the right buttons to press to keep them interested and motivated. A varied diet of group work, paired work and individual work is key.

But group dynamics are more than this; it is about establishing tolerance and empathy in the class, an equitable culture in which all efforts are recognised and personal bests are valued more than being better than everyone else in the room. Who has the most ideas rather than who has the best one? Who works the most collaboratively rather than who works the fastest? If someone finishes early, have they spent their time helping others or smugly telling others how quickly they've done it?

Living in a classroom means living in a crowd and this brings all sorts of challenges, not least for one's self-motivation. It is important to emphasise to the children that their achievement and success are not relative to others' achievements and successes, but rather it is defined by what they have done in the past and if they have improved on their efforts from last time. Are they making progress? Have they learned something?

But one cannot live in a vacuum with the kind of tunnel vision that will see you accused of not sharing or not collaborating or not recognising others' strengths. We expect children to share in each other's successes *and* remain self-motivated at the same time! The classroom is a melting pot of power, popularity and preconceptions about each other and each other's abilities, little wonder then that some children appear to lack self-motivation in this arena. Why should they feel motivated to learn their spellings this week if last week, and every week before that, the child sitting next to them achieved full marks? Or why should they feel motivated to finish the painting they began last week if, already, the painting belonging to their neighbour is turning out 'better' than their own?

Pressing on with what you've started, regardless of what others are doing is surely a difficult and robust skill for any of us to master, young or old. The man who builds his house alone on the moon will value it greatly, until the moment a new lunar resident constructs a bigger house next door to him. Just like the recluse values his paintings with which he adorns his house until he subscribes to a painters' magazine and sees others' efforts. At which point he may burn his brushes and try gardening.

How do any of us stay motivated alongside others? I suggest it is by valuing our own efforts and seeking to exceed them next time. It is always intriguing to meet a person, often around the age I am now, training for their first marathon. They don't usually set themselves the target of beating everyone else and coming first. I doubt they're interested in second place either, or tenth. What interests them more is setting themselves a personal challenge that is often far outside their comfort zone and then achieving it. But it doesn't end there. The other things that motivate first-time marathon runners, just like other middle-aged men in lycra, are the health benefits that they will experience before and after they've done it. Personal goals and personal benefits – these are the things that motivate many of us and yet often they seem counter-intuitive to being part of a team, part of a class. There is no 'I' in team as we are often reminded, though I've never much liked the phrase.

I suspect – though I have never done a marathon myself and so cannot confirm this to be true – that after the race is over, the sense of camaraderie among the runners is life-affirming. I doubt that all those runners descend into fights and arguments because some have run quicker times than others. They are able to draw on a collective sense of accomplishment, whatever their times were – not through their combined efforts, mind, but through knowing what each other has gone through to get there. They can share in something very special.

This is what we must strive for in a classroom. We should be able to celebrate others' achievements, not because ours are better (so we can afford to congratulate them), but because we know what they went through to get there. One can still draw a sense of accomplishment when surrounded by others who may also be achieving great things because collectively everyone had to overcome similar struggles and similar worries. Such camaraderie doesn't judge each other's contributions, it recognises that we're in the same boat facing the same challenges.

Goal setting

A competitive group dynamic often demotivates as many children as it motivates, perhaps more. But some pupils are very motivated by striving to be the best on their table, best in their class or best in their year group. As teachers we can be flexible in our approach and knowing your pupils is always key.

Setting goals that are achievable is the secret to keeping the children self-motivated. These can and should be personal goals, pitched at their current output and attainment levels, or just beyond them.

In his superb book, *Help Your Boys Succeed*, Gary Wilson writes on self-motivation. Although he is referring to boys exclusively, of course, his excellent advice here is just as relevant for girls too:

> We don't help self-motivation when we do everything for him. Instead we are encouraging the development of learned helplessness. Neither do we help when we encourage unrealistic expectations, since focusing on the top of the mountain often means he gives up because it always seems so far away. On the other hand, encouraging every independent thought and action and every positive move he makes in the direction of fulfilling his potential while gently rolling the carpet out a little at a time will help. (Wilson, 2008: 48)

For many children the learning objective can seem far away in the distance – a goal that others will undoubtedly reach before they do. But we can set goals that are manageable and which still ultimately lead to the summit. We want to give targets to children that will motivate them along the way. Perhaps this is why at CPD sessions I deliver on this topic, I have often proposed that we use the phrase

Assessment for Motivation in addition to Assessment for Learning, because I believe any target setting should be designed to motivate the learner to want to make progress. Such targets must, as I have said, be bespoke to the learner's needs and potential, rather than serving as a group target, as most learning objectives seem to be in class.

Setting goals for the group and for the individuals within it is only part of the story. What we also need to do is consider how we can ensure that the group dynamic of the classroom is one of peer support and encouragement. For even though there will be a wide variety of talents and abilities in the class – and the children will be all too aware of this, which may affect motivation, as I have said – there is still the chance to create a culture of support in which everyone can feel it is worth trying their best and working hard because they know that the results of their efforts will be appreciated, and they won't be eclipsed by someone else's greater talent.

Group discussions

Circle time has often featured in strategies for addressing group dynamics and climate. When conducted correctly, and if it feels safe to do so, children can and will express their views and share their concerns with one another. The focus for any circle time discussion needs to have a positive default setting – that is to say any discussion must set out to have positive outcomes for everyone. Why else would you hold a discussion in class if not to bring benefit to learning and the learners? When discussing how we feel in class, and whether we feel motivated, the positive benefits are obvious and you can set the tone by emphasising that we want to make the atmosphere in the room even more positive and supportive for everyone. In order to do this, we may consider the following questions as prompts for talk:

i.   Why does motivation matter so much?

ii. What does it feel like to be highly motivated?

iii. What is the difference between intrinsic motivation and extrinsic motivators?

iv. How and when do we feel self-motivated in class?

v.   Why do some people feel demotivated at times?

vi. What we can we do about this as a group?

None of these questions needs to result in negative exchanges. Provided this circle discussion is properly chaired by the teacher or teaching assistant, it should be illuminating for everyone. Most importantly, discussing together what makes us feel motivated or demotivated will help to build a more caring and considerate classroom, and that brings all sorts of benefits to children's intellectual and emotional development.

In his *A Theory of Motivation*, Maslow suggests that 'belongingness' is the third basic need in all of us, just above physiological and safety needs. Whether we know it or like it or not, we are essentially interdependent beings and this need must be met in classrooms too. Emphasising the benefits of a caring culture of support does not in any way reduce the opportunities for intellectual growth and development, as Carmel Cefai explains in her book, *Promoting Resilience in the Classroom*:

> The focus on social pressures in education does not weaken achievement, nor is it a distraction from learning. On the contrary, an ethic of caring is at the heart of teaching and learning, providing a foundation upon which effective learning and success can be built and socio-emotional competence developed (Noddings 1992). Caring not only fosters the socio-emotional aspect of pupils' development, it also enhances their intellectual abilities. Pupils who feel trusted and valued internalise the values and goals that the teachers hold for them and are more likely to be motivated. (Cefai, 2008: 55)

Feeling trusted and valued is essential for our intrinsic motivation to survive when we work as part of a group. There is no doubt that when we create a more caring, trusting environment and a culture of mutual respect and support, this will have a positive impact on pupils' motivation to work hard and achieve their potential. This is because we are minimising the risk of encountering derision when it goes wrong or teasing from others when it goes well. It is worth paying attention to the group's ethics and values, and underlining at every available opportunity that a prosperous classroom is built on love and respect. For me, it's a non-negotiable.

One of the barriers to children's self-motivation is injustice within the group. You will know of many children, I am sure, who demonstrate a finely tuned sense of injustice, not only for when they have been treated unfairly themselves, but when their friends have too. There is nothing so demotivating as feeling that your efforts will not be recognised or, even worse, will be mismarked or confused with someone else's efforts, or be subject to a different set of criteria and scrutiny than others' work. If it's a level playing field and everyone's work is judged against the same standards, whilst at the same time recognising personal achievements and personal goals, then most children will be motivated to work hard. The moment it seems inequitable, intrinsic motivation diminishes for many students. Why bother trying, after all?

The challenge, both for pupils and teachers alike, is to create a culture in which we support one another and recognise each others' talents and achievements at the same time as allowing everyone to feel self-motivated to do their best. Whether it is in the classroom or in the staff room, individuals' contributions need to be recognised both for what they mean on a personal level *and* for what they bring to the group as a whole. The two need not be mutually exclusive.

Put simply, do we want to be part of a team of players, all of whom are motivated to be the best they can be? The answer must surely be yes.

Synergy and conflict within the group

But even if everyone is highly motivated within a group, does this mean they will work well together and get along just fine? It is unlikely; human nature doesn't work that way, I find. It depends very much on what motivates you.

For the children who are motivated by competition and being the best in the group, they may struggle when paired with children who are demotivated by fame and acclaim; for the children who are motivated by solving problems and embracing new challenges, they may find it difficult building a working relationship with a partner who is more motivated by routine and predictable futures, someone who may be change averse; and the child who finds leading others highly motivating may struggle to understand why others in the class prefer to work independently and enjoy being a free spirit.

It's back to those circle discussions again. Tolerance and empathy are important virtues when working within a group. The children will come to understand that we all embrace challenges and tasks in different ways depending on what motivates us, but we have to do them anyway. The problem-solving task that is seen by one child as an exciting opportunity to think creatively and come up with something original may be viewed by another as a worrying break from the routine and devoid of the systems or procedures that guide them. Neither attitude is best nor worst; they just stem from different ways of being motivated.

The child who is motivated by friendship and feeling valued will work well with someone who is equally motivated by such belongingness, but pair him up with a free spirit who likes to work independently and he may struggle. Similarly, the pupil who craves attention and stardom may fail to understand why her working partner doesn't want any such glory and finds it all very embarrassing.

And some think we just pair up children based on their ability!

As I have already mentioned, too many times probably, knowing your students is paramount and will enable you to put them in the right pairings and groupings, in which they will stay motivated.

Knowing what does or does not motivate a pupil, and equally, knowing what actively demotivates them, is central to good teaching and learning. This is why I work so much with schools today to use the Motivational Map™ to identify such motivators in a quick and efficient way, so that teachers can maintain those levels of motivation in their students.

Balancing our own needs with the needs of others

It is a difficult lesson for anyone to learn, and especially a child, that for a group to work successfully and for each of its members to remain motivated, we need to balance our own needs with the needs of others; both are important.

If we want students to stay positive and self-motivated, we need to address their needs. These may come in the form of educational needs, social and behavioural needs, physical needs, psychological needs, emotional needs, and so on. We are, after all, complex organisms with different perceptions of the world around us and different ways of interpreting what we experience. Children often react very differently to exactly the same set of circumstances and surroundings. So much is obvious.

Our motivation is affected deeply by our wants and needs. Motivation is not fixed, like our character, perhaps; it is dynamic, it changes to meet the circumstances we find ourselves in and the needs we have at a moment in time. The experiences we have in our lives will affect our needs, and so in turn this will affect our motivation. It is rare for a person's motivation to be driven by the same drivers over many years.

For example, let's imagine a person finds himself in a job where he is unable to enjoy any autonomy. His employer manages every move he makes, undermines him at every opportunity, and expects to be consulted on every decision to be taken. Colleagues depending on him for decisions will soon realise this dynamic and so will go straight over his head to the employer for quick decisions; they know that this is all their line manager would do anyway, so why wait? It would be understandable for the person in these circumstances to find himself another job. When he does, his motivation will be driven by a significant need for autonomy. And this driving force, to be a free spirit, will have been heightened as a result of his previous job. His wants and needs have been influenced by prior experience and his motivation adjusts accordingly.

Children are no different. Let's imagine a child who is teased at school, perhaps for being too clever, or not clever enough, or for wearing glasses, or for having spots on her face; the list of possible scenarios is, unfortunately, endless. Let's imagine that the child – we'll call her Lucy – endures so much teasing and persistent bullying that she hates school. She doesn't try her hardest because she is too preoccupied by negative thoughts about herself, caused by the constant teasing. She doesn't work hard and consequently is rarely praised in class. She is overlooked at the best of times, chided for not working hard enough at other times.

Lucy moves to another school. As soon as she arrives in the new place, she will have a strong need for acceptance, to feel liked and valued. Every child has this need, because we all do, deep down, but in this particular case Lucy's motivation will be especially enhanced if she feels she is liked and valued and part of the team. This is as a direct result of her previous experiences. Lucy's motivational drivers have changed because her wants and needs have changed. Now more than ever, she will want to know that the problems of before won't be repeated in her new school, and in order to satisfy herself of that, Lucy will crave acceptance, friendship and being valued. If she experiences this, her motivation to join in and work hard will be greatly enhanced.

In order to boost Lucy's intrinsic motivation, it might seem reasonable to make extra effort in class to ensure she feels valued and included. Her teacher might praise her publicly; Lucy might also be encouraged to apply for a school council role, or a librarian or a classroom monitor. Others in the class will be encouraged to include Lucy in their games; and the teacher will look for every opportunity to boost Lucy's confidence and self-esteem by celebrating her achievements in class and in assembly.

And looking on, throughout this whole restorative process, is Jen, the child sitting next to Lucy.

Jen has already gone off Lucy. It's nothing she's done, just that up until she arrived, Jen was the popular one. She was the one with the most friends, the most house points and the most mentions in assembly. She was the star, and it motivated her to be so.

Who's right and who's wrong? Who's more important? Whose needs take priority?

Clearly, every good teacher would know not to exclude Jen when supporting Lucy. It is, of course, possible to welcome Lucy into the group and boost her confidence whilst not disenfranchising Jen. But you can see how there is some balancing to be done here. And this is only two children – many classes have thirty in them, sometimes more.

6 Choices and challenges

There has been plenty of thought already in this book on how we can make challenge appealing and motivating for children in school. The greatest rewards lie outside of our comfort zones, but so too does the greatest motivation, I believe. There is a sense of accomplishment to be found in working towards and ultimately achieving a goal that is challenging. It's why mountaineers climb, after all. Motivation needs a challenge in order to flourish. How can a child feel motivated to do something if it is easy and well within their comfort zone?

Perhaps this is why a significant number of high-achieving children lack motivation in school: because they do not find the work challenging enough, or the tasks are not sufficiently open-ended to allow for some differentiating up, to stretch them and allow for extension work.

Differentiating to meet pupils' needs, as we know, can often focus primarily on supporting and scaffolding the lower attainers. Able children can all too easily be provided with more of the same work, so we are differentiating by outcome, by sheer volume of work rather than ability or challenge. This is rarely motivating for the able child and of very limited value in terms of learning, other than to keep the children quiet and on task.

Challenge is needed for everyone. With robust optimism securely in place and the kind of grit and resilience that we all talk about in schools today, and rightly so, it is possible to keep the learning challenging for everyone so that motivation can thrive. Pitching tasks just beyond children's current attainment levels or output can keep them striving to achieve more rather than settling for doing the minimum required and sailing through school with A grades but never really being intrinsically motivated. And it is a requirement of the DfE's Teachers Standards, of course, that we keep the children challenged. A teacher must:

> Set goals that stretch and challenge pupils of all backgrounds, abilities and dispositions. (DfE, 2011: 10)

Facing up to a goal that has been specifically designed to stretch and challenge you requires courage, a growth mindset and plenty of robust optimism. Encouraging pupils, just like staff, to leave their comfort zones and have a go at a difficult challenge is seldom easy. When it comes to having the motivation to do so, the key issue for me is *empowerment*.

Empowerment as a motivating force

Empowering children to step up and believe they can take on a challenge is what education is all about. How else can we prepare them for life? Empowerment implies enablement but it also implies having the licence, or permission, to take things on yourself, the freedom to have a go. Empowerment is so important for the motivated learner. But it requires a very real sense of ownership – a feeling that what you do can and will make a difference, that your contribution will matter.

I have already mentioned that children need to feel the work they are producing is *their* work, that they are doing it for themselves, rather than for some external reward or simply to please the teacher. If we are to build a 'no-excuses culture' – and avoid that blame game when things go wrong and pupils, or teachers, don't perform well – then we need to encourage them to feel a sense of self-control. The best way to do this is by providing them with choices as often as we can, at the same time as encouraging them to feel *empowered* to make decisions and be responsible for the consequences.

Most children respond well to independent projects. This is why many enjoy topic lessons in the afternoon more than they enjoy English or maths lessons in the morning! Lessons taught around a theme – 'The Victorians', 'Space' or 'Fashion', for example – often involve creative projects in which the children are given an element of choice in how they work and what they produce. The perimeters set seem wider somehow, more creative and with no fixed prototype for what must be produced. They may be asked to produce a research project, put together a presentation, draw some designs, or compile a newspaper article or fictional diary about a given event witnessed or a famous life lived. Tasks like these bring with them opportunities for some independent choices to be made – for content, form, design and layout, authorial voice, style and so on. At each point in the design process a decision needs to be made and this can be liberating and motivating for many children, especially those who are particularly motivated by having some autonomy.

But of course this need not be limited to topic lessons only or for arts and humanities. There are numerous opportunities in all subjects for the children to feel they have some creative space in which to make a choice, use some initiative and bring some originality to the task.

As teachers we can often lose motivation when we feel we have no choice in our work, no autonomy; when there is no room for error and no room for interpretation. Very few colleagues I have ever worked with have enjoyed being micro-managed by their line manager or headteacher. Such prescription can be demotivating for many of us and when the element of choice and challenge is removed – albeit because our over-efficient line manager is trying to 'support us' – then we can often lose our motivation to perform to the best of our ability. We become automatons. The same is true of the children. We want them to feel a sense of responsibility and ownership in their learning, because we know this will encourage them to feel motivated and have a positive attitude. As referred to in earlier titles in this series, such aims are encompassed in the aforementioned DfE's Teachers Standards, of course. A teacher must:

Encourage pupils to take a responsible and conscientious attitude to their own work and study. (DfE, 2011: 10)

In the 'MORE learning' model I referred to in Chapter 4, motivation often comes from a sense of ownership. Every task set, no matter how prescriptive it may seem, can bring with it opportunities for the children to make a choice, and not just the right or wrong choice.

There has been a move in recent times to offer more creative tasks for homework, often presented to children in the form of a grid of optional projects for them to choose and then run with. As much as I don't like homework *per se*, I like this. Anything that gives the children some freedom to choose a task, rather than being set a task, and then provides an open brief that can be interpreted creatively and individually must be a good thing.

It is worth reviewing your planning to see how many tasks that are being completed in class and at home involve elements of choice and challenge for the children. How many of them are designed simply to check that the children have grasped a concept or skill? The latter is important too, of course, but we must recognise that these tasks in themselves may not be motivating for the children; rather, the more creative, open-ended and independent projects will ultimately help us to raise children's interest and motivation, precisely because they involve some choices to be made.

Problem-solving tasks are often enjoyable and motivating for pupils because they involve elements of choosing, trial and error and independent thinking. These are empowering elements for the motivated learner.

Making independent choices

Not all children find difficult challenges motivating. But this may not be because of the challenges themselves; it is more likely to be because of some insecurity some children may be harboring about their own ability, or lack of it. If all children had confidence in their own ability and belief that their efforts will be valued, then I believe all children would be equally motivated by challenge. We are, as a race, motivated by the quest for answers about ourselves and about the world around us. We are most motivated when we are working towards a challenging goal, whatever it may be for us. If we are not motivated by such things, it may be because we don't believe we'll like the answers we find or we don't believe we are good enough to succeed in our efforts. But we are.

When you think about it, and encourage the children to think about it too, it is surprising how many choices the children have made before they even pitch up at school. What order do they get dressed in? Do they brush their teeth before washing their face? Do they eat toast or cereal, or both? What juice do they prefer? Do they spend the last precious minutes before setting off to school completing their homework, which they chose not to complete the night before, or watching SpongeBob Squarepants on television, or reading a book, or hunting for their school shoes, or winding up their little sister?

Reminding children of the choices they make on a daily basis will help them to realise that, contrary to what they probably believe, they do enjoy a lot of choice in their lives already – granted, some children will be given more choices than others. They do possess the skills needed to make independent decisions and have done since they were old enough to think and express their preferences. The most demotivated children I have taught often believe they have no choice in their lives, everything is arranged for them and they 'have no rights at all!' It will always be the preserve of children to complain about their lack of freedom and independence, and some more than others! It is only when we are adults, with responsibilities and mortgages or rents to pay, that we feel nostalgic for the carefree days of childhood. But it didn't appear to us at the time that we had so much freedom.

To motivate any person, whether a child or an adult, one needs to highlight for them the choices they have and the permission they have been granted to make those choices, within reasonable boundaries. Failure to recognise this permission will only lead to a corrosive and demotivating blame culture, where they feel they have no choice and therefore cannot be blamed when things go wrong. The demotivated teacher will often be the first colleague to blame others for their own poor performance.

I try to give colleagues freedom to make choices in their own roles, whether it be through the lessons they plan, the displays they produce or some other aspect of their roles and responsibilities. There is nothing so enjoyable as being asked by a motivated teacher if they can initiate some new project, club or activity for the children – and being able to say 'Yes, go for it!' Such a conversation can only come after time spent empowering staff to step up and feel in control, giving them licence to be creative whilst at the same time ensuring they are fully aware of the school's policies and the standards expected! The same is true of children: explain the standards and expectations we have for them, clearly and concisely, and then allow them to get on with it and see what they can really do.

What is school for? Is it to impart established knowledge which children will need to learn in order to thrive in the world beyond school? Or is it to reveal to them the endless choices and challenges in the world and then to encourage them to have enough self-confidence, discernment and self-motivation to step up and participate?

Or is it both?

7

The element of doubt ∴

When we set out on a creative task we are rarely certain of its outcome. We could be the most confident, self-motivated person, but we don't really know if what we are embarking on will be an unequivocal success, and this, I suggest, is the most motivating part of it all. When we put pen to paper, when we compose, design, construct, or engage in any form of human endeavour, there always remains that small element of doubt that it will turn out as we hope. Will our efforts have been worth it? Will we 'succeed'?

For me, such risk can be a motivating force. This is why I struggle to find motivation long after I have proven I can do a job and everything has become comfortable and routine. I don't do consolidation years in my career; I can't coast. The good news is, there isn't a school anywhere that reaches this moment of perfection when there is nothing left to do, so it is okay to be motivated by new challenges and changes if you are in the teaching profession; no two years are the same. And no teaching job is without its challenges, even if you've been doing it for years.

But I realise that not every adult and not every child is like me. I am not better than them; I am not worse. I am just me. It motivates me to engage in difficult challenges that carry some risk, some element of doubt. That is not to say I am foolhardy or reckless, far from it. Where children are concerned, I am as meticulous as any teacher must be when risk assessing and ensuring the safety and well-being of my pupils. But in my own career, as in my own life, I like to take on things that are difficult, out of my comfort zone. I like the unknown. But some adults, and many children, don't. Or at least, they think they don't.

In actual fact, I believe everyone likes the thrill of the unknown to some extent; it's what makes us human. It is not the unknown we fear, it is our perceived inability to cope with what's coming that fills us with dread sometimes. Helping colleagues and students to manage change, as any school leader will tell you, is fraught with challenges – perhaps that is why I enjoy it so much, because it is so challenging and because it requires every interpersonal skill one has and every ounce of emotional intelligence and empathy we possess.

Embracing doubts with confidence!

Recognising an element of doubt in our work, or in situations we find ourselves in in our lives, is not the same thing as having doubts about our ability. The presence of an element of doubt in tasks and ventures we embark on can, and should, motivate us to do our best. But possessing doubts in ourselves: that is less motivating.

To stay motivated, children need to feel confident that they will, or could at least succeed. If they have significant doubts about their own ability, so much so that they believe they could never succeed at a particular challenge, then it is unlikely they will be able to find the motivation required even to start it. So whilst an element of doubt can spur us on and motivate us to have a go (enticed by the tantalising prospect of succeeding against the odds), this only works if we are feeling confident.

How does all this translate to the classroom and the teaching and learning that happens within it? As ever, it is about making sure the children feel confident before they embark on a difficult task; it is about reminding them that they do indeed have the skills and knowledge required to have a go. It is also about encouraging them to see that when things get tricky, when they are in the 'learning pit', this is when things become exciting and when real learning takes place. 'Being stuck' is all part of the learning process; how we respond when we are stuck, that's the important part, and it should be motivating for the confident learner. As Piaget said, 'intelligence is not what you know but what you do when you don't know.'

I should explain what I mean by 'element of doubt' here so that it does not confuse. When a child embarks on a problem-solving activity, there should be no doubt in their mind about their own ability to complete it; they have the requisite attitudes for learning – grit, optimism and resilience, for example – because we as teachers have worked on these, modelled them and encouraged them to grow in the children (see *Teaching for Character* earlier in the series). It is the solution to the problem that may be shrouded in uncertainty – and that is just the point. Without an element of doubt here, there would not be a problem so it is not a problem-solving activity! It is the lack of certainty as to where the solution lies that should be motivating for the child, if we have prepared them well enough. And it is this element of uncertainty, or mystery, that should be motivational.

Investigative learning

When the answer to a problem or a learning task is already revealed to the child before they have even embarked on it is, I would argue, when demotivation sets in – there is, after all, nothing left to investigate, and yet it is the investigating that is the exciting part. Certainty removes the need to investigate. We have all taught able children who have already perceived an answer very quickly and therefore become bored and unmotivated. For these children especially, an element of doubt is very important. As Paul Claxton writes in his much-quoted *What's the Point of School?*, schools can often act as if knowledge is more certain than it really is:

> Brave teachers could take up the idea that was suggested by the late Neil Postman, an American critic of conventional education. We know, he said, that knowledge is essentially uncertain – an always tentative, always improvable product of fallible human intelligence. And we know that much of education acts as if knowledge were more certain than it is. Teachers, textbooks and syllabuses use too much unjustified 'Is' language and not enough 'Could Be'. So his idea was to appoint the class as a whole to be detectors and investigators of overblown claims to certainty. They are to become Knowledge Investigators. (Claxton, 2008: 159)

I think this is tremendously motivating for children. The idea of encouraging them to become knowledge investigators, out to scrutinise and test others' claims to certainty, is excellent. It affords the student the chance to see for himself if the knowledge is indeed true, to assume there is an element of doubt which needs investigating further.

Learning is finding out for oneself whether something is true or not. It is a motivational experience, or should be. Reading, assimilating and remembering the indubitable knowledge of others is less motivating, surely, though important too.

But it would be in the realms of fantasy to suggest that every syllabus now needs to rip up the established lessons of past thinkers and experts in their field just so that children can find it all out for themselves! It would be difficult not to accept that gravity exists, for example, or that 25 times 2 is indeed 50. But we can sell these things to children in such ways which allow them to decide for themselves if what they are reading and watching and hearing makes sense *to them*. Does it sound reasonable? How might the theorists have come up with these theories in the first place? What can the children experience in their own lives that might corroborate or refute these established theories? They may have been around for centuries in some cases, and believed and accepted by generations of people ever since, but if the child is encountering this 'established' knowledge for the first time then it is not established until they have established it for themselves! This is the motivating aspect of learning, the investigative process, if you will.

No child wants to believe that everything that can be proven has already been proven and that everything that can ever be known is already known – and that the only role left for them is to read, remember and regurgitate (what I often call the 3Rs) the canon of knowledge that others have discovered and proven.

Certainty can be the death of motivated, investigative learning. What's left is just rote.

But we are living in an exciting, and worrying, era of uncertainty. The combination of rapid technological advances bringing all sorts of ethical and moral questions, redefining how societies function, fears over climate change, and the depletion of the world's natural resources at a time when global population is soaring, all make for an uncertain future for the world and us. It is this uncertainty that makes deep learning possible and essential in schools today. We have both a mandate and a responsibility to encourage children to question, scrutinise, experiment and think creatively like never before. One would not want to suggest that we educators are rubbing our hands with glee at the current problems of the world, precisely because of the rich learning opportunities they present, but it is an undeniably exciting and motivating time to be involved in education.

A concise summary of how the role and nature of teaching and learning in schools has changed over time because it has had to, is offered by Rob Stokoe in his excellent book, *Leaders of Learning*:

> Throughout the 18th and 19th Centuries, education developed around the notion of supporting the development of the industrial revolution, retraining students coming from an agrarian economy and instilling discipline, punctuality, concentration and the ability to receive information, learning was a process of acquiring. Education was separated into small testable bits and then assessed. Today we are facing changes regarding how we learn, what we learn and where we learn. The journey our young learners are travelling will not allow us to teach them all they need to know because we cannot with certainty determine what that future will be. (Stokoe, 2014: 60)

8 Observation

What are the indicators that a child is feeling motivated? How do we know? Do we look at their grades? Does an A* mean that the student is highly motivated and therefore does an E grade mean they are not?

To use attainment data to tell us whether a child is or is not motivated is to leave it too late. The low grade may be a consequence of a child feeling demotivated, just as a high grade may come from high motivation, but this is by no means the whole picture. There are, as ever, myriad other factors and influences to consider, all of which make up a child's learning performance, and, as I have argued before in this series, conflating results with performance is never a good thing.

Identifying the observables

The key to this is knowing and recognising the observables in play when the child is learning – knowing what to look for and then extrapolating evidence from it. How we observe children's motivation, and how we report on it, is of paramount importance in education, since it is a student's motivation that will have greatest impact on her success, ultimately.

Boys' tongues usually stick out when they are feeling energised and motivated, and caught up in the fury of writing. One could record how many times a boy sticks his tongue out during a lesson, perhaps?

Can you imagine? What would that child's report look like? 'In Science, Nathan has been working hard this term and has been very motivated; he achieved a tongue sticking out average (TSOA) of 35 seconds per minute. Impressive.'

There must be other ways of observing children's motivation than looking at their tongues.

Work rate is one such indicator. A child will be prolific if engaged in, and motivated by, a subject or topic. They will think more, write more and produce more ideas. Their class book will not be peppered with half-finished pieces and empty pages. They will probably require a new book before anyone else!

Care and attention to presentation and neatness is another indicator – and conversely the demotivated child will care less about the presentation of their work. Handwriting, I find, is often an accurate observable when it comes to motivation. I can see it in my own children's homework. When lacking motivation and being ordered to complete their homework by their father, my boys especially will pay less attention to the quality of their handwriting – and you can see the peaks and troughs clearly in their books. A conscientious approach to homework does seem to require high levels of motivation, of the *intrinsic* kind; external rewards, such as the promise of time on their Xbox, seem to lead to rushed and often incomprehensible writing!

Another indicator of motivation levels is the extent to which a child will participate in class discussions and ask questions. The demotivated student is less likely to ask insightful questions, other than 'Why do we have to do this?' Conversely, when a child is self-motivated and feeling engaged in a subject, she will share opinions and ask for clarification readily, precisely because she is motivated to complete the work and complete it well.

One of the quickest ways to see if a child feels motivated is quite simply by looking at his eyes; you can see them sparkling with interest, dancing with the delight of getting stuck into something they find exciting and challenging. A motivated student will look at things straight on, not from the side, peering from the corner of his eyes, holding something back. He will properly focus on things, rather than gaze or glance. He will frown and screw up his eyes, whilst thinking and internalizing carefully what it is that holds his interest. Demotivated children prefer to look at the floor, or at the desk, or anywhere apart from where you want them to look, and least of all at you!

Talk is another accurate measure of motivation, I find. The motivated student will find all sorts of things to talk about but the child who lacks self-motivation will often remain quiet and reticent.

Some motivated children take pride in their appearance too, dressing smartly and taking care to look good. They are punctual and usually have everything they need with them in class. They are motivated to do well, to try their best, and this means having the correct equipment with them, rather than forgetting and borrowing or making any excuse not to do the task in hand because they don't have the right equipment!

All this is not to say that the motivated child is convenient to teach and the unmotivated child is not! Often highly motivated children can be chatterboxes, or finish too quickly or rush and miss important things. They require careful managing, they talk a lot and they can sometimes distract others or upset them by setting themselves up in competition with them. The child who lacks motivation will often happily sit quietly and not contribute to the lesson at all, causing no distraction and no trouble. But most of us, as teachers, are not motivated by such a quiet life; rather, we want to make a difference, we want children to learn and to grow and develop. We take a pro-active stance and we don't settle for half measures or children 'opting out' of a lesson because it doesn't interest them or because they lack confidence. We want everyone to feel the buzz of learning.

Observing learning habits

There are many schools these days that recognise the need for myriad observables of progress and development other than grades and percentages. Some schools call it 'habits of mind', others use terms like 'learnability' or 'learning attitudes'. Any system that helps teachers to observe and report on their students' learning performance as well as the results of that performance is a good thing in education and it needs to be encouraged more. This is because when we shed light on these learning attitudes and aptitudes (what I call 'invisible ink') we are getting much closer to assessing a child's motivation levels than we ever are by looking only at his grades. The following, then, is a list of behaviours, or 'learning habits', that can be observed, the result of which will give you a fair indication of the child's current motivation levels. I have suggested a score of 1 to 10, though you could also use RAG rating (red, amber, green) or letters A-E.

Learning habits	1 – 10
Work rate and output in class	5
Contributing to class discussions and talking partners	6

Care and attention to presentation	4
Willingness to edit and improve their work	3
Responding positively to marking and feedback	5
Punctuality and preparedness for lessons	6
Positive attitude and self-belief	5
Energy levels and enthusiasm in class	6
Showing resilience when mistakes are made	4
Keenness to try new challenges	3
Total score	47

Figure 5: learning habits for monitoring motivation

The above score of 47% suggests that this child's current motivation may be low – because if it were higher the learning behaviours seen in class would each receive higher marks. It would be difficult to work hard, respond positively to feedback and take care with presentation, for example, if the child were lacking self-motivation. Remember this is not a value judgement about attainment or ability, so it is not true to infer that this child may still be highly motivated but is scoring low marks because of their innate ability (like a child can score a high grade for effort and a low grade for attainment on some traditional reports or assessment cards, for example). The learning behaviours listed here don't work that way. They have everything to do with motivation rather than innate ability or intelligence. They are concerned with work rate and attitude and a general willingness to have a go – and these are inextricably linked to motivation, I would argue. So we can infer from the total score that this child's motivation must be low at the moment. We can observe it – or we can observe the consequences of his low motivation in class.

By giving this child a score of 47%, we are not saying he is failing; rather we are using this score to show us, as teachers, that we need to do more to raise his motivation, based on the learning behaviour he is showing, so that, in turn, his learning performance, and his attainment levels, will rise.

Whenever we put marks against a child's name, they can so easily be interpreted as a judgement. When it comes to behaviours, attitudes and in this case motivation, we need to ensure that such marks are not interpreted in this way, not least because they can have the opposite effect to the desired one – they can even work as self-fulfilling prophecies when they are seen as an achievement report. Such a list of observations is just that – *observations* by the teacher to inform the way she will meet this child's needs in future, so that he may gain more motivation and become a more engaged, resilient learner. They are not assessments. They shed light on learning performance which in turn sheds light on that most invisible but arguably most impactful element in a child's learning – their *motivation* to learn and succeed.

9 Conclusion

We cannot force someone to be motivated, just as we cannot coerce someone to be curious or creative or possess any other quality or attitude that makes up their 'invisible ink'. What we can do is create the conditions in which children will feel motivated. When we value motivation, it happens around us. We build a motivating learning environment. As model learners we can, and should, present a positive, hopeful disposition. Such a growth mindset will always win over the cynics and take on those rare few who are motivated by demotivating others. There is no place for cynicism or defeatism in education. There is only optimism. An unshakeable belief in children's potential will always give rise to motivation and positivity.

In Ian Gilbert's *Essential Motivation in the Classroom* (2002), he cites a charming story of a little girl who is asked by a visiting inspector if she can swim. She replies, 'Yes, but not yet.'

This story fills me with hope, because it is about hope. I marvel at the little girl's robust optimism. Of course she will learn to swim. And this attitude will, I am sure, give rise to her motivation to do so. If you want to raise motivation in learning you need to saturate the children's minds with a wash of hope. We can all get better, be better people and find better success. The only thing holding us back is a lack of hope, which is all too quickly replaced with apathy and demotivation.

The school in which I am currently Headteacher is a school that, despite being in special measures and despite suffering all the ignominies of poor Ofsted inspections in the past, is a very hopeful and motivating place to be. Our robust optimism and our hope will carry us through, I am certain (along with a great deal of hard work, which we feel motivated to do).

Every morning, I open the door to a charming little girl who is dropped off at our breakfast club earlier than any other pupil. She always greets me with a smile when I open the door and welcome her in, even when it's raining.

Her name is Hope.

References

Blandford, S. (2015) *Make School Better*. Woodbridge: John Catt Educational Ltd.

Cefai, C. (2008) *Promoting Resilience in the Classroom*. London: Jessica Kingsley Publishers.

Claxton, P. (2008) *What's the Point of School?* Oxford: Oneworld Publications.

Covey, S. (1999) *The 7 Habits of Highly Effective Teenagers*. London: Simon & Schuster UK Ltd.

Department for Education (2011) *Teachers' Standards*.

Gilbert, I. (2002) *Essential Motivation in the Classroom*. London: Routledge Falmer.

Kohn, A. (1999) *Punished by Rewards*. New York: Houghton Mifflin.

Maslow, A. H. (1943) *A Theory of Human Motivation*. Eastford, CT: Martino Publishing.

Peters, S. (2012) *The Chimp Paradox*. London: Vermillion.

Sale, J. (2016) *Mapping Motivation*. Farnham: Gower Publishing.

Stokoe, R. (2014) *Leaders of Learning*. Woodbridge: John Catt Educational Ltd.

Wilson, G. (2008) *Help Your Boys Succeed*. London: Continuum International Publishing Group

Also Available

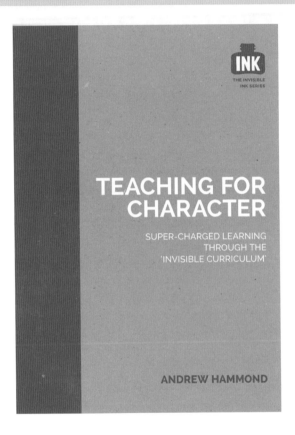

"This book ought to be mandatory reading for all who want to nurture the thinking and learning of children and young people (and adults if it comes to that, just think what it would do to a professional development day)."

Max Coates, UCL Institute of Education

Order online from
www.johncattbookshop.com
£10

Also Available

"Andrew Hammond shows that opportunities for creative responses lurk everywhere – in any lesson and around the lessons ... hugely informative, lively, engaging – and yes, creative."

Geoff Barton, Secondary headteacher and educational author

Order online from
www.johncattbookshop.com
£10

Forthcoming titles in the Invisible Ink series

Teaching for Curiosity

Teaching for Thinking Skills

Teaching for Communication

Teaching for Interdependence